In Memory of
Bob Callagy

A Dedicated Friend
of the Rye Free
Reading Room

JANE AUSTEN

LITERATURE AND LIFE: BRITISH WRITERS
Selected list of titles in this series:

W. H. AUDEN	Wendell Stacy Johnson
ANTHONY BURGESS	Samuel Coale
NOEL COWARD	Robert F. Kiernan
ARTHUR CONAN DOYLE	Don Richard Cox
T. S. ELIOT	Burton Raffel
FORD MADOX FORD	Sondra J. Stang
E. M. FORSTER	Claude J. Summers
OLIVER GOLDSMITH AND RICHARD BRINSLEY SHERIDAN	Marlies K. Danziger
ROBERT GRAVES	Katherine Snipes
GRAHAM GREENE	Richard Kelly
ALDOUS HUXLEY	Guinevera A. Nance
CHRISTOPHER ISHERWOOD	Claude J. Summers
JAMES JOYCE	Bernard Benstock
KATHERINE MANSFIELD	Rhoda B. Nathan
CHRISTOPHER MARLOWE	Gerald Pinciss
JOHN MASEFIELD	June Dwyer
W. SOMERSET MAUGHAM	Archie K. Loss
V. S. NAIPAUL	Richard Kelly
BARBARA PYM	Robert Emmet Long
JEAN RHYS	Arnold E. Davidson
SHAKESPEARE'S COMEDIES	Jack A. Vaughn
SHAKESPEARE'S HISTORIES	George J. Becker
SHAKESPEARE'S TRAGEDIES	Phyllis Rackin
MURIEL SPARK	Velma Bourgeois Richmond
TOM STOPPARD	Felicia Hardison Londré
J. R. R. TOLKIEN	Katharyn W. Crabbe
EVELYN WAUGH	Katharyn W. Crabbe
OSCAR WILDE	Robert Keith Miller
VIRGINIA WOOLF	Manly Johnson
WILLIAM BUTLER YEATS (PLAYS)	Anthony Bradley
THE POETRY OF WILLIAM BUTLER YEATS	William H. O'Donnell

Complete list of titles in the series available from the publisher on request.

JANE AUSTEN

June Dwyer

A Frederick Ungar Book
CONTINUUM • NEW YORK

1989

The Continuum Publishing Company
370 Lexington Avenue
New York, NY 10017

Printed in the United States of America

Library of Congress Cataloging-in-Publication Data

Dwyer, June.
  Jane Austen / June Dwyer.
    p.   cm. — (Literature and life series)
  "A Frederick Ungar book."
  Bibliography: p.
  Includes index.
  ISBN 0-8264-0448-0
  1. Austen, Jane, 1775–1817—Criticism and interpretation.
I. Title. II. Series.
PR4037.D88 1989   89-32360
823'.7—dc20   CIP

For Quetzal and Colin

Contents

Acknowledgments

This is a book with virtually no citations of secondary sources. The amount of critical material written on Jane Austen is enormous and doing it justice would have meant writing another book. Austen's novels have inspired a number of excellent studies. Those works that are often cited in Austen criticism and those books that I personally have found most enlightening are listed in my Selected Bibliography. I am very much indebted, as is anyone who writes on Jane Austen today, to R. W. Chapman's masterful 1925–54 edition of her novels and minor works and to his 1932 edition of her letters. While I was writing this book, Park Honan's new Austen biography appeared. With its many new facts and fresh insights, this work was immensely helpful to me.

I would like to thank Evander Lomke, my editor at Continuum, for his patience and encouragement during this project. I am also most grateful to my colleagues in the Manhattan College Dante Seminar for their lively discussion, comments, and queries about my essay on *Persuasion*, a part of which was presented in that forum. To my colleague and friend, Robert Kiernan, I owe an enormous debt. He read my manuscript, challenged my ideas, questioned my expression, and corrected my syntax with grace and good humor. A final word of praise and thanks to Eleanor Moulding, my eleventh-grade English teacher, who made me memorize the first line of *Pride and Prejudice* and first showed me how to appreciate Jane Austen.

Chronology

Dec. 16, 1775	Jane Austen born at Steventon Parsonage, Hampshire.
1783, 1785–86	Austen sent away to school in Oxford, then Reading with sister Cassandra.
1790–93	Juvenilia written and shared with family.
1795	First draft of *Sense and Sensibility* (called *Elinor and Marianne*) written.
Spring 1795	Cassandra engaged to Thomas Fowle.
1795	*Lady Susan* probably written.
Dec. 1795	Austen's flirtation with Tom Lefroy.
Jan. 1796	Austen's surviving correspondence begins.
Oct. 1796 to Aug. 1797	First draft of *Pride and Prejudice* (called *First Impressions*) written.
Feb. 1797	Cassandra's fiancé dies in the West Indies.
Nov. 1797	*Sense and Sensibility* begun.
Nov. 1797	*First Impressions* offered to Cadell & Davies for publication; offer declined.
1798–99	*Susan* (*Northanger Abbey*) written.
Spring 1801	Austen's father retires and moves his family to Bath.
Summer 1801	Austen meets clergyman in Devon whom she is expected to marry; he dies.
Dec. 1802	Harris Bigg-Wither proposes to Austen; she accepts, then refuses the next day.

1803	*Susan* (*Northanger Abbey*) sold to Crosby & Co., but never published.
1804	*The Watsons* begun.
Jan. 1805	Austen's father dies.
1807–9	Austen, Cassandra, Martha Lloyd, and Mrs. Austen live in Southampton with brother Frank and his new wife.
April 1809	Austen writes Crosby about *Susan's* nonpublication; is told she may repurchase manuscript.
April 1809	The Austen women and Martha move to Chawton Cottage, Hampshire on brother Edward's estate.
Feb. 1811 to Summer 1813	*Mansfield Park* written.
Nov. 1811	*Sense and Sensibility* published.
Jan. 1813	*Pride and Prejudice* published.
Oct., Nov. 1813	Second editions of *Pride and Prejudice* and *Sense and Sensibility*.
Jan. 1814 to Mar. 1815	*Emma* written.
May 1814	*Mansfield Park* published.
Aug. 1815 to Aug. 1816	*Persuasion* written.
Dec. 1815	*Emma* published.
Dec. 1815	*Susan* finally bought back from Crosby.
Feb. 1816	Second edition of *Mansfield Park*.
Summer 1816	Austen's health begins to fail.
Jan. to Mar., 1817	*Sanditon* written.

May 1817	Austen moved to Winchester in effort to cure her illness.
July 18, 1817	Austen dies of Addison's disease.
Winter 1817–18	*Persuasion* and *Northanger Abbey* published.

JANE AUSTEN

1

Family and Fiction I:
Jane Austen's Life

Unlike her fictional heroines, Jane Austen never wed, and it is largely due to this fact that we have the six remarkable novels that make up her oeuvre. She began writing seriously in 1795 at the age of nineteen when she was—to put it crudely—still marriageable. Had she taken a husband in the next five years, it seems unlikely that anything she wrote would have been published. In an 1817 letter to her niece Fanny Knight, Austen strongly suggests that marriage stifles a woman's imagination: "Oh! what a loss it will be when you are married. . . . I shall hate you when your delicious play of Mind is all settled down into conjugal & maternal affections."[1] Suspicious though she was about marriage's effect on women, she remained fascinated with the subject of courtship throughout her literary life. All of her novels deal with the difficulties and the pressures of finding an appropriate mate, and they all suggest that conjugal felicity is possible. It belittles Austen's achievement, however, to state simply that she devoted her considerable talents to writing about how women find husbands. Her focus is human nature; courtship is simply the lens through which she viewed it.

Austen wrote about the society in which she lived, avoiding the farfetched, the bizarre, and the foreign. She herself had many experiences, however, that she chose not to explore in her fiction. Her second brother George was mentally retarded, but his illness is alluded to only once in the family correspondence, and nowhere in her fiction is such a disorder mentioned. Neither does death occur in Austen's work. During her lifetime, loved ones and relatives succumbed to fevers, accidents, even the guillotine, but no one dies in her novels.

In trying to match Austen's experiences to her fiction and in studying her omissions to ascertain whether they stem from a lack of knowledge or a wish to avoid certain topics, the reader quite forgets how little is actually known about the author's life. Two very good Austen biographies have been written in recent years: the short *Jane Austen: Woman and Writer* by Joan Rees (1976) and the more encompassing *Jane Austen: Her Life* by Park Honan (1987). Each brings with it new insights and new facts, but until considerably more solid information about the author herself is uncovered (a most unlikely event), there will never be a "definitive" biography. Right now too much is missing. One feels the silences created by letters that were lost or destroyed and by the vagueness of certain stories that became part of the Austen family lore.

Austen's first biographers were her family members, and despite the blinders of love and awe that they wore while regarding their increasingly famous relation, they served her well. Among them, the best was James Edward Austen-Leigh, the son of her oldest brother, who wrote a *Memoir of Jane Austen* in 1870, which he expanded in 1871. He was eighteen when his aunt died and the only member of his generation to attend her funeral. Fifty years later in what he termed his "old age" he decided to "rescue from oblivion any events of her life or any traits of her character to satisfy the enquiries of a generation of readers who have been born since she died."[2] The memoir includes personal reminiscences, social and historical observations, selected letters, portions of unfinished works, and a discarded ending for Austen's last finished novel, *Persuasion*.

Critics and scholars have since emended some of Austen-Leigh's information and added to both his aunt's biography and her published oeuvre, but their debt to him remains substantial. Although sometimes sentimental and uncritical of "dear Aunt Jane," many of his observations are astute and admirably expressed. Generalizing about how Austen passed her time, he writes,

Of events her life was singularly barren: few changes and no great crisis ever broke the smooth current of its course. Even her fame may be said to have been posthumous: it did not attain any vigorous life until she had ceased to exist. Her talents did not introduce her to the notice of other writers, or connect her with the literary world, or in any degree pierce through the obscurity of her domestic retirement.[3]

A number of enthusiasts have tried to counter Austen-Leigh's assessment, saying that Austen's life was not so very quiet, that she was well aware of politics since two of her brothers were in the navy, and that her letters indicate an awareness of a much broader spectrum of social behavior than she ever chronicled in her novels. While all this may be true, her days still come across as uneventful, even dull. The important events took place in her mind. Jane Austen's life may be reduced to two key circumstances: she never married and she wrote novels.

Austen was born into the kind of family about which she so often wrote. At the time of her birth in December of 1775, her father George Austen was a middle-class, small-town clergyman who held livings in the Hampshire parishes of Steventon and Deane. George Austen and his wife, Cassandra Leigh, had wealthy relations, but they never enjoyed the ease that adequate wealth can bring. Although rarely spoken of directly or protractedly, money worries were always a part of the Austens' life. The family was a large one, the author being the seventh of eight children. She remained close to several of her siblings all her life, but the bond between her only sister Cassandra and herself was particularly strong. They went to school together briefly and then were educated by their father at home. They always shared the same bedroom, and when separated by visits to friends and relatives, they corresponded regularly.

Cassandra became her sister's chief caretaker when in 1816 Austen contracted Addison's disease, a kidney disorder that killed her within a year. After the ordeal was over, she wrote to her niece Fanny, "I *have* lost a treasure, such a Sister, such a friend as never can have been surpassed,—she was the sun of my life, the gilder of every pleasure, the soother of every sorrow, I had not a thought concealed from her, & it is as if I had lost a part of myself."[4] Even allowing for the idealizing tendency that the death of a loved one brings, the reader senses that Cassandra's devotion to her sister was exceptionally strong. She has, however, often been cast in the role of ogre by critics and biographers who fault her for destroying a number of apparently personal letters from her sister. There is no question that she was more concerned with Jane Austen's privacy than with her fame. However, the fact that her actions indicate devotion rather than impersonal literary vision is scarcely blameworthy. Had she saved all of Austen's letters with an eye to publication, critics no doubt would have faulted her for a mercenary instinct.

Fame, even of the most modest sort, was unthought of by Austen during most of her life. Her aim, like that of her sister and most of the young women in her class, was to marry—to find love and financial security by finding the proper husband. On one occasion, the young Austen jokingly filled out a parish register form engaging herself to the fictional "Henry Frederick Howard Fitzwilliam of London." Another parish document of her authorship boasted her supposed marriage to "Arthur William Mortimer of Liverpool."[5] An acquaintance of Austen's during these years remembered her as "the prettiest, silliest, most affected, husband-hunting butterfly," an assessment that, if not quite true, at least gives one a sense both of the author's youthful high spirits and of her desire to marry.[6]

When Cassandra became engaged to the Reverend Thomas Fowle in 1795, Austen probably assumed that she, too, would soon find a husband. Fowle, however, died unexpectedly in the West Indies in 1797, and although Cassandra recovered from the blow, she never married. Ironically, Austen's fate was to be similar to her sister's. In December of 1795 a youthful flirtation occurred between herself and Tom Lefroy, the visiting nephew of one of the Austens' neighbors. Although she was interested in Lefroy and joked in a letter to Cassandra about his proposing, nothing of the sort actually happened. In fact, he may have been sent away to deter his growing interest in his lively, but relatively poor new acquaintance. Lefroy had no fortune of his own and his family wanted him to marry money—something the Austens could not offer him. Indeed, fifteen months after his departure from Hampshire, he became engaged to an Irish heiress. This turn of events evidently wounded Austen, who a year and a half later was still "too proud to make any enquiries"[7] about him in conversation with his aunt.

A few years after the flirtation with Tom Lefroy, two other prospective suitors appeared in Austen's life. The first, the Reverend Samuel Blackall, professed a wish to know the author better, but she was not inclined to encourage him. Self-important and overbearing, he may have become the model for Mr. Collins in *Pride and Prejudice*. In 1801 a second, considerably more important suitor made the author's acquaintance. Details are sketchy, but apparently Austen met an attractive young clergyman while vacationing with her family on the Devon seacoast. The Austens approved of him, and although the two young people kept company for only a few weeks, the family's expectation was that they all would meet again soon and that he would propose marriage. The reunion never occurred; instead, a letter arrived from the man's brother with news of his death. The episode remains vague, repeated among members of succeeding generations of Austens without further particulars—not even the man's name. With no direct reference in the author's extant letters to this unhappy episode, the measure of its true importance is impossible to gauge.

There is record of only one actual proposal of marriage that Austen received. At the end of 1802 when she was almost twenty-seven and living with her family in Bath, she hastily agreed to wed Harris Bigg-Wither, a former Steventon neighbor who was six years her junior. Within twenty-four hours, however, she had changed her mind. Although Austen was attached to the young man's sisters, he himself was far from appealing. Tall, uncouth, and taciturn, he lacked social grace, owing probably to a troublesome stutter. Austen's initial acquiescence poignantly demonstrates the pressure young women of her class and fortune felt to marry even without affection. In this case, however, the author's independent spirit triumphed, and she was able later in life to advise her niece Fanny not to accept meekly her first offer of marriage. All of Austen's novels reinforce her behavior and her advice: with the exception of Elinor Dashwood, every one of her heroines receives an unwelcome proposal of marriage, and every one of these unacceptable offers is rejected.

Having decided against a marriage to Harris Bigg-Wither and apparently receiving no other proposals, Austen remained with her family for the rest of her life. Indeed, after the two brief periods between 1783 and 1787 when she and Cassandra were little girls away at school, she was never to live apart from her relatives. She traveled very little—only around the south of England to visit other family members and friends. Her Hampshire home meant a great deal to her, and when her mother announced without preamble in early 1801 that the family was moving to Bath, Austen became badly upset. As Reverend Austen was seventy years old at the time, the family's relocation to a fashionable gathering place may have been a last-ditch effort to find husbands for the unmarried daughters.

The Austens' five-year stay in Bath did not prove happy. The author felt acutely her family's lack of wealth and the condescension of the well-to-do toward those of modest means. Events of early promise quickly faded. Austen's marriage prospects had dimmed with the death of her attractive clergyman suitor and her refusal of the Bigg-Wither proposal. She wrote little; the fragment now known as *The Watsons* was begun in Bath. The manuscript of her novel called *Susan* (later to be transformed into *Northanger Abbey*) was sold to a publisher in 1803, but never put into print. Finally, in early 1805 Reverend Austen died quite suddenly, leaving the author, her sister, and their increasingly hypochondriac mother with very little income.

In 1807 the three Austen women and their good friend, Martha Lloyd, who had joined their household in Bath, moved to Southampton where the fifth Austen son, Frank, had taken up residence with his new wife. Frank was a captain in the navy and between commissions at the time his family joined him. Although the arrangement was a decided improvement on the Austens' life at Bath, the two and a half years the four women spent in Frank's Southampton household were claustrophobic and difficult. Finally, in the fall of 1808, the third Austen son, Edward, invited the women to live on one of the two estates he had inherited from the wealthy Knight family who had raised him and made him their heir. His offer was prompted by the death of his wife Elizabeth after the birth of their eleventh child. Relations between Elizabeth and the Austen women had been cool, but a move near Edward's now-motherless children seemed suddenly to everyone's advantage.

Given the option of a cottage at Godmersham in Kent or one at Chawton in Hampshire, Mrs. Austen preferred the latter, a choice that the author heartily endorsed. During her eight-year absence from Hampshire, Austen had missed the quiet countryside where she had been raised and had begun to write. Her talent thrived at Chawton. When she moved there in 1809, she was an unpublished author; eight years later, all six of her novels were in print, three of them written entirely at Chawton and the others revised and polished there. The combination of a settled home environment and a receptive public proved a great stimulus to her talent. Austen's death in 1817 interrupted a period of remarkable creativity.

The writing career that ended prematurely in Hampshire had begun there some twenty years before with a similar burst of creativity. Between 1795 and 1798, the young Jane Austen wrote drafts of several books. The first was probably her short epistolary novel now called *Lady Susan*. The extant manuscript of the novel is a copy made by the author in 1805 during her stay in Bath, but the style of the work suggests an earlier composition date. James Austen-Leigh included *Lady Susan* in his 1871 *Memoir,* but the work never had a literary life of its own. In contrast, another epistolary novel, *Elinor and Marianne,* written a little later than *Lady Susan,* was to manifest considerable literary vitality. In 1797 the author reformulated the story without the clumsy letter apparatus and renamed it *Sense and Sensibility.* It was the first of her novels to be published—although many years were to elapse between its completion in 1798 and publication in 1811. As none of the drafts or revisions of the work now exist, scholars can only speculate how much polishing of the original occurred over the thirteen years that the novel remained in manuscript.

Henry Austen handled the negotiations with publisher Thomas Egerton to have *Sense and Sensibility* printed and continued thereafter as his sister's literary agent. Although Austen apparently was reluctant to publish the novel, once she was in London to correct the proofs all of her doubts disappeared. Responding to her sister's inquiries about the book, she declared, "I am never too busy to think of *Sense and Sensibility*. I can no more forget it than a mother can forget her suckling child."[8] The responsibilities of authorship agreed with her. The book did remarkably well. Its first edition sold out in about eighteen months, and a second edition was commissioned in 1813. Among the novel's readers was the Prince Regent's fifteen-year-old daughter, the Princess Charlotte, who found the appealing, but overly romantic character of Marianne Dashwood "very like in disposition" to herself.[9] Amid these stirrings of literary recognition, the author remained anonymous; the title page simply stated that *Sense and Sensibility* was By A Lady. Austen seemed content in her anonymity. On writing to their niece Fanny, Cassandra included a warning not to "mention that Aunt Jane wrote '*Sense and Sensibility*.' "[10]

Like *Sense and Sensibility*, Austen's second published novel, *Pride and Prejudice*, was also begun in the late 1790s. Initially known as *First Impressions*, the book was written between October of 1796 and August of 1797. Shortly after its completion, Reverend Austen with very good intentions, but not much literary perspicacity, had tried to interest the publishers Cadell and Davies in the book. His letter contained no description of the story, but only announced that he had in his possession "a Manuscript Novel, comprised in three Vols. about the length of Miss Burney's *Evelina*" that he would be happy to allow the gentlemen to peruse.[11] Never has Austen's work been more limply introduced. Messrs. Cadell and Davies declined the offer.

First Impressions remained in the author's possession, often read and enjoyed in family groups over the next decade. The idea of publishing the work was never wholly abandoned, for in a letter to her sister, Austen joked, "I would not let Martha read 'First Impressions' again on any account. . . . She is very cunning, but I saw through her design; she means to publish it from memory, and one more perusal must enable her to do it."[12] Publication finally came in early 1813. After *Sense and Sensibility*'s success in 1811, *Pride and Prejudice* was welcomed by Egerton. The title was changed because another novel named *First Impressions* had appeared in 1799. The story, too, underwent a number of revisions over the years; no one really knows how many. In a letter to Cassandra, Austen refers in particular to her having "lopt & cropt" the manuscript shortly before its publication.[13]

The positive reception of *Pride and Prejudice* made Austen expansive. Both she and her family enjoyed the praise lavished on the book by admirers who had no way of knowing that the anonymous author was one of their acquaintances. Austen herself confided to Cassandra that she thought Elizabeth Bennet "as delightful a creature as ever appeared in print."[14] The public agreed and bought up the first edition of fifteen hundred copies in six months. A second edition appeared in the fall of 1813; a third, in 1817.

The third of Austen's novels written in the 1790s, *Northanger Abbey,* had a more convoluted publishing history than either *Sense and Sensibility* or *Pride and Prejudice.* Originally called *Susan,* it was, according to the author's sister, written "about the years 98 & 99" shortly before the family left Hampshire for Bath.[15] Austen's literary efforts abated during the time of her residence in Bath, but in 1803 Henry Austen was able to sell *Susan* to Crosby and Company for the modest sum of ten pounds. The book was advertised but never appeared, probably because Crosby also published Ann Radcliffe's *Mysteries of Udolpho.* Austen had mentioned that book's capacity to lead untutored minds astray in her work, and Crosby was apparently fearful of undermining the reputation of one of his best sellers. In 1809, when Austen was about to leave Southampton for Chawton, she made an effort to ascertain the status of *Susan.* Writing the publisher under the pseudonym "Mrs. Ashton Dennis," she inquired whether the manuscript might not have been lost and offered a second copy only if it were quickly seen into print. She received a prompt answer saying that she might repurchase the manuscript for the original sale price and advising her that their agreement had included no promise of publication. Without money to spare and about to move again, Austen left the matter as it was. The manuscript was finally retrieved in late 1815 when Austen's fame and her finances made the step desirable. As Henry Austen did the negotiating and *Susan*'s title page announced only that the author was A Lady, Crosby and Company did not know until after the sale how valuable a property they had let go.

The work underwent some revision. Austen changed both the heroine's name and the book's title, but she set the manuscript aside early in 1817, telling her niece Fanny, "Miss Catherine [the novel's heroine] is put upon the Shelve for the present, and I do not know that she will ever come out."[16] Austen had nevertheless prepared an explanation of the book's history for its prospective readers:

This little work was finished in the year 1803, and intended for immediate publication. It was disposed of to a bookseller, it was even advertised, and why the business proceeded no farther, the author has never been able to learn. That any bookseller should think it worthwhile to purchase what he did not think it worthwhile to publish seems extraordinary. But with this, neither the author nor the public have any other concern than as some observation is necessary upon those parts of the work which thirteen years have made comparatively obsolete. The public are entreated to bear in mind that thirteen years have passed since it was finished, many more since it was begun, and that during that period, places, manners, books, and opinions have undergone considerable changes.[17]

The work was not published until six months after the author's death, and the awkwardness of the ending argues that Austen had probably not finished her revisions even though she had penned her introduction.

Nowhere are the gaps in Austen's biography more frustrating than in the history of the manuscripts of her first three novels. Interestingly, she preserved a number of her juvenile writings dating from 1790 in three notebooks. The lack of strict chronology of the dated pieces in the notebooks, together with the neatness and uniformity of the copy, indicates that the works were recopied and, one assumes, edited in some way. If, as the inclusion of one letter dated 1809 indicates, these juvenile writings were compiled when the author was thirty-four, she probably did some judicious editing, changing, or omitting what was dull or overly silly.

Although most readers would have little interest in changes made in 1809 to Austen's five-page picaresque spoof entitled "Henry and Eliza," the same could not be said for her revisions of the manuscripts of her first three novels. The changes that transformed *Elinor and Marianne, First Impressions,* and *Susan* into *Sense and Sensibility, Pride and Prejudice,* and *Northanger Abbey* are a subject of considerable curiosity. These early manuscripts were probably discarded when the revised works were purchased for publication. Their recovery, although unlikely, would be a most welcome event.

In contrast to the complicated evolution of Austen's first three novels, the development of the last three, which were written at Chawton, was smooth and uneventful. One niece recalled watching her aunt there:

Aunt Jane would sit quietly working, saying nothing for a good while, and then would suddenly burst out laughing, jump up and run across the room to a table where pens and paper were lying, write something down, and then come back to the fire and go on quietly working as before.[18]

The author had just begun *Mansfield Park* early in 1811 when *Sense and Sensibility* was sold to Egerton, an event that must certainly have bolstered her confidence. By the time she had completed *Mansfield Park* in July of 1813, the first edition of *Pride and Prejudice* was being eagerly bought up and widely enjoyed. Events could not have been more propitious for the new book: it had a willing publisher in Egerton and a ready audience awaiting it. Austen's name was still not on the title page, but readers were anxious to buy a book identified to be By the Author of *Pride and Prejudice. Mansfield Park* appeared in May of 1814 and the first edition was sold out by November. Nevertheless, the book did not cause much excitement. It was very different from *Pride and Prejudice,* and Egerton, sensing there would be little interest in a second edition, did not offer Austen the option.

The author kept a personal record of her family and friends' responses to *Mansfield Park* that is both informative and touching. While prefiguring many modern reactions to the story and its characters, the document also affords the reader a glimpse of the obvious delight Austen took in her accomplishment. Almost everyone has something positive to say. The younger and less inhibited family members tended to dislike the book's very proper heroine, Fanny Price, and generally to prefer the story of *Pride and Prejudice*. Austen's lively niece Anna "could not bear Fanny" but very much liked the officious Mrs. Norris and the unruly Price family at Portsmouth.[19] The author included her publisher Thomas Egerton's praise of the book's "morality" in her list, as well as the inane (and truly Austenian) comments of one Mrs. Augusta Bramstone, who "owned that she thought S.& S.—and P.& P. downright nonsense, but expected to like M. P. better, & having finished the first vol.—flattered herself she had got over the worst."[20]

Still basking in the approval of her family and friends, Austen kept a similar record of reactions to *Emma* when it came out at the close of 1815. She had completed writing the book in only fifteen months, and Henry had found her another publisher, John Murray, who would also reissue *Mansfield Park*. The new book was dedicated to the Prince Regent, whose chaplain, the Reverend James Clarke, had invited Austen to visit the royal library at Carlton House when she was in London awaiting the proof sheets. Suspecting that the visit was tantamount to a request for a dedication, Austen inquired and was told that the gesture, although not necessary, would be welcome. She had little use for the Regent—indeed, he embodied many of the qualities she ridiculed in her novels, for he was pompous, spendthrift, and dishonorable. But she understood her duty and dedicated *Emma* to him just the same. The dilemma was not unlike Fanny Price's dutiful submission to authority in *Mansfield Park*, and Austen undoubtedly appreciated the irony of the situation.

Although the reissue of *Mansfield Park* was almost totally ignored, the first edition of *Emma* sold out within a year, helped by a long and admiring assessment in the influential *Quarterly Review*. The anonymous reviewer turned out to be Sir Walter Scott, and his observations were remarkably astute. He likened Austen's art to "the Flemish school of painting [whose] subjects are not often elegant, and certainly never grand; but they are finished up to nature, and with a precision which delights the reader."[21]

Honored though she must have felt by Scott's praise, Austen still wrote to Murray (who published both *Emma* and the *Quarterly Review*) complaining, "I cannot be but sorry that so clever a man as the Reviewer of *Emma* should consider [*Mansfield Park*] as unworthy of being noticed."[22] Even though the public and the great Sir Walter Scott manifested little interest in her third published novel, the author still held *Mansfield Park* in high esteem.

As she wrote to defend her least popular literary offspring, Austen had yet another novel almost complete—*Persuasion*, begun in August of 1815 and finished the following August. While she was still at work on *Persuasion*, her health had slowly begun to fail. Nevertheless, between August of 1816 and March of 1817, when her painful kidney disorder entered its final stages, Austen polished *Persuasion*, did some revision of the *Northanger Abbey* manuscript, and began a new novel. Only in reading accounts of her steadily worsening illness in the first three months of 1817—the same period during which she was writing the remarkable *Sanditon* fragment—does one begin to appreciate fully Austen's stamina and the depth of her talent. At the end of March, she finally became too ill for literary work, but she still penned letters and light verse. Her family moved her to Winchester in May, hoping specialists there might save her. But her condition worsened, and on July 18 she died, with her head cradled on Cassandra's lap. She was only forty-one years old.

Austen was buried in Winchester Cathedral. Her family placed a plaque there that flattered her character, while only vaguely alluding to her literary talents. Citing nothing more specific than "the extraordinary endowments" of Austen's mind, the inscription dwelt instead on her "charity, devotion, faith, and purity." Fifty-five years later, a new generation of Austens put a second plaque on the cathedral wall. Reflecting the author's growing reputation, it began with the words, "Jane Austen, known to many by her writings," before passing on to her other virtues. The modesty of this inscription is somehow appropriate to the modesty of the author's life. It does not begin, however, to suggest the tremendous impact that Jane Austen had on the history of English literature or on the lives of so many millions of readers. The author would have appreciated the irony of the tribute.

2

Technique and Theme
in the Novels

Everyone loves Jane Austen's novels—scientists, feminists, college freshmen, traditionalists, even readers who think they don't like fiction. After Shakespeare and perhaps Dickens, Austen is the most universally admired writer in the English language. Her popularity is extraordinary when one considers that she deals with neither death nor religion nor great moments in history. Her subject is courtship and her stories all end the same way—in happy marriage. Yet no one has ever accused Austen of being shallow or suggested that her novels appeal because of their escapism. Quite the contrary—her work is usually characterized as wise, witty, and realistic.

In many ways Austen's novels resemble Shakespeare's comedies, which also end in marriage. Both the novels and the comedies demonstrate how much human nature may be revealed within the confines of a circumscribed environment and a limited plot. Like Shakespeare, Austen makes women her central characters. By using their wits and their moral sensibilites as a substitute for the power they do not have, they bring about a desired end. This element in itself—the success of the weak over the powerful—may account for some part of Austen's popularity.

The greater part of Austen's appeal, however, is rooted in her ability to combine the seemingly incompatible qualities of romance and irony, engagement and detachment. Rational though she may initially appear from the beauty of her balanced sentences, there is much in Austen's work that is firmly rooted in the realm of the feelings. Despite her elevation of civility, restraint, good manners, good sense, and duty, Austen's novels are essentially fairy tales—fantasies. They are grounded in realism and made credible by careful observation and sound precepts of moral behavior, but they are fantasies nevertheless.

With the exception of Emma, Austen's heroines are never beautiful. They are attractive but not exceptional young women with whom readers can readily identify, and their stories are the stuff of daydreams, where the ordinary person wins the elusive, longed-for mate. In the manner of all durable human fantasies, Austen's fictions are never quite complete. The hero finally declares his love in moving and flattering terms, but the heroine's reply is never dramatized. In *Emma* Mr. Knightley begins his proposal saying, "If I loved you less, I might be able to talk about it more," and then he goes on to explain himself. But of Emma's reply, Austen's narrator observes only, "What did she say? Just what she ought, of course." With the climactic moment never fully drawn, the fantasy never ends, and as a consequence, it invites replaying.

The lack of physical description in Austen's novels—from what a character is wearing to the color of his or her hair—also encourages the readers' participation. The author's descriptive adjectives are rarely concrete: Mr. Bingley is "good-looking and gentlemanlike [with] a pleasant countenance and easy, unaffected manners" while his friend Darcy draws attention to himself by his "fine, tall person, handsome features, noble mein." This is standard fare in Austen; the descriptive words she picks are general, abstract, and often morally weighted. The author manipulates her readers' judgment through the inclusion of words like *noble* and *gentlemanlike,* but they must fill in most of the physical particulars. In so doing, readers find themselves further enmeshed in the stories.

No one likes to admit that Austen's novels might be the author's own personal fantasies—a series of daydreams created by a woman who would readily have married a man like any one of her heroes. Yet, on some level, the novels are the author's fantasies. Insofar as Austen particularizes her heroines, they all bear a resemblance to her—indeed seem to be described only in terms of those features that contemporaries have recalled as memorable in

Austen herself. Austen's lively dark eyes, good complexion, and upright figure recur in most of her heroines. Not one of these young women has blue eyes; neither do they possess features such as straight noses or oval faces that were not peculiar to Austen.

But if Austen is making a statement about her own condition in her novels, she is also saying something about the human condition. Readers respond to the fantasies in her novels because they are commonplaces and address the human need for love and respect. Realism broadens the appeal of the works by making the romance seem authentic. However, romance still presupposes personal engagement in the story, an identification of the readers with the hero and heroine. If Austen's novels were only realistic romances, they would be limited by their lopsided appeal to the emotions. Her considerable use of irony, however, counterbalances this overcloseness. It distances the readers from involvement in the story so that they identify with the narrator as well as with the characters. Where Austen's romance engages the emotions, her irony appeals to the wit and reason.

The range of this irony adds to its power. With quick mastery, Austen can deliver herself of a single mock-serious statement, as in the well-known opening of *Pride and Prejudice:* "It is a truth universally acknowledged, that a single man in possession of a good fortune must be in want of a wife." Or she can belittle human folly by an accretion of deftly turned sentences, like those that mark the less familiar, but equally skillful beginning of *Persuasion:*

Sir Walter Elliot, of Kellynch-hall, in Somersetshire, was a man who, for his own amusement, never took up any book but the Baronetage; there he found occupation for an idle hour, and consolation in a distressed one; there his faculties were roused into admiration and respect by contemplating the limited remnant of the earliest patents; there any unwelcome sensations, arising from domestic affairs, changed naturally into pity and contempt . . . and there, if every other leaf were powerless, he could read his own history with an interest which never failed.

Sometimes Austen lets her wit cut too deeply. Her remarks on married women's abilities to talk of nothing but their children in

Sense and Sensibility and her dismissal of the worthless Dick Musgrove in *Persuasion* seem overly cruel. But she also has the ability to mock gently at the faults of flawed but decent individuals like Miss Bates in *Emma* and Mrs. Jennings in *Sense and Sensibility*. She is most unrelenting and usually at her best with those characters like Sir Walter Elliot in *Persuasion* and Lady Catherine de Brough in *Pride and Prejudice* whose social pretentions and inflated sense of worth make them society's most uncivil members.

Two categories of people escape her irony altogether—those who are gently good and those who are dangerously bad. The kind and retiring personalities of Fanny Price, Jane Bennet, and Jane Fairfax cannot sustain ironic treatment without being destroyed, and so Austen lets them alone. Conversely, an ironic treatment of manipulative characters like George Wickham, Lucy Steele, and William Walter Elliot would have softened their sinister personalities by making them funny instead of threatening. So they, too, escape Austen's wit.

Austen's irony allows her to poke fun at people and ideas through overstatement and understatement. Because her criticism is indirect, it is readily accepted by her readers. This irony also creates a relationship between the narrator and her readers; her wit telegraphs information to them about which the characters have no conception. This intimacy is not one of sharing secrets so much as it is the holding in common a repertory of private jokes. The appreciation of Austen's irony binds her readers to her narrators, just as the romance of her stories engages readers with her characters.

The themes that recur in Austen's novels are considerably more far-reaching than descriptions of her plots would suggest. Several of her novels address the loosening of rationalism's hold on English society and the advent of Romanticism. It is important to remember that *Sense and Sensibility* was being written about the same time that Wordsworth and Coleridge brought out the seminal document of English Romanticism, the preface to the *Lyrical Ballads*. There is no indication that Austen ever read the poems or the preface to the ballads, but a new attitude was in the air, and she tried to counter it in her fiction—firmly at first and then with less and less conviction. Those tenets of Romanticism that particularly affected her were its tendency to celebrate the individual isolated from society, its preoccupation with the power and grandeur of nature, and its elevation of the emotions over reason.

Northanger Abbey scoffs at the excesses of pre-Romantic gothic fiction, showing that an imagination unchecked by reason will inevitably go astray. Through Henry Tilney's urbane wit and good sense, the novel's heroine, Catherine Morland, is weaned from her fascination with the antisocial and overly charged emotional situations of such works as Mrs. Radcliffe's *Mysteries of Udolpho*. Catherine is a sensible girl at heart, and so the gothic is never a genuine threat to her character. Henry's attention works as an incitement to send her down a path upon which she is already inclined to travel.

The sentimental excesses of gothic novels were easy marks for Austen, but the serious claims of Romanticism proved more troublesome for her to dismiss. In *Sense and Sensibility* she creates a situation where a sympathetic character, Marianne Dashwood, falls passionately in love with John Willoughby, whom she considers the ideal lover—her soul mate. Totally absorbed in this solitary and exclusive passion, she behaves uncivilly and irrationally to everyone else around her. When Willoughby suddenly withdraws his affection, she has no resources and falls into a state of nervous collapse. Austen convincingly illustrates in *Sense and Sensibility* the dangers of too great a reliance on feeling and too strong a belief in the exceptional nature of the individual. Marianne learns that there is no single soul mate for her and ends by entering into a happy marriage with a man who bears no resemblance whatsoever to the once-irresistible Willoughby.

When Austen wrote *Sense and Sensibility,* she was unaware of how appealing Marianne Dashwood was going to be to her readers. For many of them, Marianne's spirit and her willingness to fly in the face of social convention was much more attractive and sympathetic than her sister Elinor's rationality. However, by the time Austen came to write *Mansfield Park,* she was more fully aware of the seductiveness of the Romantic personality—even as it exposes itself to ruin. In that novel she delineated the insidious appeal of the artistic and Romantic personalities of Mary and

Henry Crawford. Unlike Marianne Dashwood, whose behavior is innocent and oblivious, the attractive Crawfords appear calculating and perfectly well aware of the consequences of their careless attitudes toward social convention. Their knowing ways signal danger to the reader, and as a result, their Romantic qualities, although still appealing, are no longer sympathetic.

By the time she got to *Persuasion,* Austen had further modified her attitude towards Romanticism. In this novel, she created a heroine who is rational and critical of Romantic excesses but who is also pining for one man whom she has loved and had to give up. Anne Elliot will not compromise when other suitors present themselves; she cannot forget her first love, Frederick Wentworth. Although Austen orchestrates Anne's story so that she is able to marry Wentworth after all, there is such sadness and such an aura of near tragedy in the book that the reader can feel the author imaginatively considering an alternative ending. Anne Elliot could very easily have been left heroically alone and isolated from the society that has failed her—a truly Romantic figure.

This drift of Austen's mind towards an acceptance of some of the tenets of Romanticism makes the *Sanditon* fragment all the more intriguing. Mr. Parker, one of the story's comic secondary characters, is—like Captain Benwick in *Persuasion*—foolishly and excessively taken by Romantic notions. Abandoning the snug and attractive house of his ancestors, he builds his family a new residence on an exposed hilltop, where one feels—as he puts it— "all the grandeur of the storm." His wife sees this grandeur in other terms, as she speaks of being "literally rocked in our bed" during a recent tempest. Austen finds laughable such Romantic excesses as Mr. Parker's, but one wonders whether the completed *Sanditon* would not have continued in the direction of *Persuasion,* granting further consideration to life's tragic elements that were recognized by the Romantic movement.

The Romantics' freedom from many worn-out social constraints appealed to Austen on some level: her novels are populated with characters—mostly women—who are unhappy with the narrow set of possibilities open to them. For all the validation of marriage that her happy endings bring, Austen still has a number of intelligent women referring matter-of-factly to matrimony as a necessity rather than a desirable end. The unspoken complaint is not against marriage itself but against a woman's lack of options. In *Emma, Pride and Prejudice,* and the fragment known as *The Watsons,* female characters speak strongly and directly about how, without husbands, they have neither security nor position in society. Only wealth, as Emma points out, can save an unmarried woman from loss of status. Elizabeth Watson eloquently states the predicament:

> ... but you know, we must marry—I could do very well single for my own part—A little company and a pleasant ball now and then, would be enough for me, if one could be young forever, but my father cannot provide for us, and it is very bad to grow old and be poor and laughed at.

The tone of acceptance in these observations is more affecting than outright protest and signals a true powerlessness.

In Austen's novels, a woman's response to the frustration of this lack of freedom is either forebearance or illness. The men who are frustrated may withdraw, move around, even run away, but the women must stay put—and either collapse or endure. In almost every novel, one or more of Austen's women characters takes some kind of refuge in poor health. Illness is a void that Marianne Dashwood falls into because of her total commitment to Willoughby. Mrs. Bennet's nerves in *Pride and Prejudice* and Lady Bertram's lassitude in *Mansfield Park* are reactions to their boredom and powerlessness. Even Anne Elliot, who stoically fights her disappointment in love, shows some manifestation of poor health in her loss of color and looks. Although Austen mocks some of her characters' adherence to poor health, she recognizes it as a psychological condition to which even strong individuals fall prey. In *Persuasion* she has the sensible and healthy Mrs. Croft articulate the causes of this condition. The good lady confesses to physical complaints of her own that appeared when she was left alone while her husband was at sea.

Austen explores the relationship between illness and dependence in almost every one of her novels. Although some of her women resist physical collapse, the author makes clear that strong character is not enough to keep a woman free from illness. What

will assure her well-being, however, is the combination of an independent spirit and an independent income. Emma is described
by her former governess and good friend, Anna Weston, as "the
complete picture of grown-up health." Her condition is generated
by the happy combination of her self-assurance and her enormous
wealth. Emma understands the strength of her position, matter-
of-factly explaining to her protégé Harriet Smith that no one will
make fun of her if she chooses to remain unmarried: her wealth
affords her a place in society that no woman of modest means
could expect. Two of Austen's heroines who have little wealth—
Elinor Dashwood and Elizabeth Bennet—actually manage to
maintain their health and to earn respect in society. They must,
however, endure many slights and work much harder to gain the
respect that is Emma's from the start.

Austen's heroines always end by marrying men of wealth, and
the health of these matches is partially posited on material security. This attitude of the author's toward money may initially appear conservative; it is certainly at odds with the Romantic
notion of the heroic common man, whose spirit transcends his
poverty. But Austen is primarily interested in the effect of wealth
on young women, who, unlike men of means, are not jaded or
hardened by its possession. Austen saw wealth as liberating
women, bringing them privileges that men—even men without
wealth—had always enjoyed.

Because a woman's lack of wealth makes her dependent on her
family, Austen spends a great deal of time exploring family relationships. If marriage is the ending of every Austen novel, the
family is the beginning. Three or four families in a country village were, Austen told her niece Anna, "the very thing to work
on"[1] in a novel—a kind of microcosm. In Austen's work, the
drama within a single family mirrors the world at large. Besides
the predictable tensions and affections, Austen's families share
several qualities that are peculiar to her worldview. The most no-
ticeable is a lack of wisdom in the older generation. Parents and
guardians of the heroines more often than not show poor judgment and little insight. From Mr. and Mrs. Bennet to Sir Thomas
and Lady Bertram to Sir Walter Elliot and Lady Russell, Austen
repeatedly demonstrates that her heroines know better than their

elders. This condition tends to undermine traditional family hierarchy. The young women behave dutifully to their parents and guardians, but the greater degree of moral wisdom resides within themselves. Although their families shelter them, they do not offer guidance. With neither family wealth nor wisdom to aid them, the success of these young women becomes a further tribute to their inner strength.

The support that Austen's heroines gain from family comes only from members of the same generation. Marianne Dashwood has her sister Elinor; Elizabeth Bennet, her sister Jane; and Fanny Price has her brother William. And interestingly enough, the men whom Emma Woodhouse, Fanny Price, and Catherine Morland eventually marry behave at first as if they were the young women's brothers. Indeed, the fraternal bond is at the center of Austen's universe. The closeness that is possible between sympathetic siblings becomes the model for the emotional ties of a happy marriage. *Mansfield Park* demonstrates this attitude most concretely because Fanny actually marries a blood relative—her cousin Edmund. As further evidence of the closeness of the two kinds of love, Fanny's delight in her brother William evokes a sexual envy in Henry Crawford that causes him to fall in love with her. Austen's insistence on the confluence of fraternal and conjugal love was probably fostered by her strong attachment to her sister Cassandra and her projection of that closeness—the only kind of closeness that she knew—into marriage.

For whatever reason, the relationship between parents and children in Austen's fiction is a mirror of the increasingly ineffectual hierarchy of the outside world. Parents fail Austen's heroines in their traditional authoritative role, just as the aristocracy had begun to fail a newly industrializing England. In contrast, family relations between members of the same generation are the model for the intimacy of a strong marriage and suggest the virtues of a more democratic bond. The failure of Austen's older generation is felt most keenly in *Persuasion* where Anne Elliot has no sympathetic siblings or close friends. In her isolation, she looks longingly at the brotherly closeness of the navy families.

The decorum with which Austen's heroines behave—especially to their elders—differentiates them from the novels' narrators, who are arch, critical, and sometimes nasty. Austen's two most outspoken heroines, Elizabeth Bennet and Emma Woodhouse, are extremely clever but keep their wit in check. The one time Emma oversteps the boundary of good taste and makes a slighting remark to Miss Bates, she is immediately chastened by Mr. Knightley and quickly regrets her cruelty. Austen's narrators, however, like the author herself, do not retract their petty cruelties. Her letters attest to her personal capacity for more than an occasional malicious observation, and they underline the tension in her books between clever characters and clever narrators.

Austen fully understood that wit and irony carry with them no inherent morality. Her ambivalence about clever speech comes out in her choice of heroines, more than half of whom are reserved and sensible young women. Appealing though Elizabeth Bennet and Emma Woodhouse may be, they are the exceptions in Austen's fiction. She purposely seems to have created the clever and amoral Mary Crawford in *Mansfield Park* as a warning to her readers (and perhaps to herself) about the dangerous charms of wit. Even Austen's male characters reflect her ambivalence toward clever speech. Her early creation, Henry Tilney, is witty and wise, but a later Henry—Henry Crawford—is not. He uses his charm and wit to serve himself alone, careless of those others whom he wounds along the way. Sidney Parker in *Sanditon* promises to be amusing, but where his wit will lead him is unclear as the fragment breaks off. Yet, one suspects that, in a reversal of the Elizabeth-Darcy relationship, the book's heroine, Charlotte Heywood, will act to curb Sidney's exuberant irony.

Austen's worry about the double edge of cleverness underscores her profoundly moral sensibility. In the end, her books are not about marriage or family or the advent of new social attitudes as much as they are about behaving well and making the right choices. People respond to Austen's stories because, inevitably, they find themselves testing their own values against them. The author, in a letter to her nephew, likened her fiction to a "little bit (two inches wide) of Ivory on which I work with so fine a Brush, [producing] so little effect after much labor."[2] But rather than belittling her subject, Austen's small scale works to elevate the lives that are being examined. The amount of labor she invests in analyzing everyday situations flatters her readers, most of whose lives are also rooted in everydayness.

Walter Scott recognized the value of Austen's familiar situations and the human scale of her work in his review of *Emma:*

Upon the whole, the turn of this author's novels bears the same relation to that of the sentimental and romantic cast, that cornfields and cottages and meadows bear to the highly adorned grounds of a show mansion, or the rugged sublimities of a mountain landscape. It is neither so captivating as the one, nor so grand as the other, but it affords to those who frequent it a pleasure nearly allied with the experience of their own social habits.[3]

Scott's understanding that Austen's novels are allied with her readers' personal experiences may finally explain the breadth of her appeal.

This appeal has extended far beyond Austen's nineteenth-century middle- and upper-class audiences. In the 1980s, a professor whose students were predominantly inner-city black men and women remarked that she had taught *Pride and Prejudice* for over fifteen years to consistently appreciative classes.[4] She found that her students enjoyed reading about an orderly society where personal choices matter and moral values are important. The notion that what a person says counts for something was of particular importance to these students—whose lives were not at all orderly and whose choices did not seem very important to anyone. Most twentieth-century readers respond with a similar wistfulness to the moral order that reigns in Austen's novels. The romance and the humor and the changing worldview all contribute to the enjoyment of her reading public, but it is Austen's insistence that individual actions matter that is, in the end, her most irresistible quality.

3

Northanger Abbey: The Need for Guidance

Although *Northanger Abbey* is the earliest and the least perfect of Jane Austen's published novels, it affords perhaps the best introduction to her worldview and to her style of writing. For the very reason that the book is too hurried in some places and too harsh in others, the reader is able to see Austen's potential and her preoccupations clearly. Less subtly set forth than her later and more polished works, this first novel illustrates especially well Austen's penchant for ironic distancing and her fondness for the innocent and morally correct individual. In none of her other work is the narrator's tone so blatantly mocking and the heroine's character so touchingly naive as in *Northanger Abbey.*

Yet it would be a mistake to consider the book a dress rehearsal for the impressive Austen productions to come. In itself the story contains considerable complexity and interest. It suffers not because of what it is but because of what comes after it. The plot centers around seventeen-year-old Catherine Morland's trip to Bath in the company of her neighbors, the Allens. There she makes the acquaintance of two very different families, the vulgar Thorpes and the more reserved and well-bred Tilneys. Each family represents a possible model for her own life: one is superficial and excessive; the other, refined and measured. Catherine's venture to Bath and then on to the Tilneys' estate of Northanger Abbey is paralleled by the inner journey that she makes as she crosses over from the world of youth and fantasy to that of complex, adult life.

This inner journey constitutes something of a triumph for Catherine, for many women in Jane Austen's novels never mature; they remain childlike and dependent, preoccupied with little-girl games like tea parties and dress-up. Catherine's neighbor and chaperone, Mrs. Allen, is just such a child-woman. She has a limited set of interests and little if any moral sense. Her compass is fixed only on the niceties of dress so that, although she is harmless to Catherine, she is also useless to her both as a confidante and a role model. Needing advice about how to behave with the rude and insistent John Thorpe, Catherine addresses Mrs. Allen in vain: "I always hoped you would tell me, if you thought I was doing wrong." Her chaperone responds that she *has* advised Catherine; she told her not to buy sprigged muslin when they arrived in Bath. Catherine's reply is both a cry for help and an indication of her inherent, although undeveloped good sense: "But this [problem with Thorpe] was something of real consequence."

Northanger Abbey explores the kind of guidance a young woman growing up in the confines of parochial nineteenth-century English society has available. Catherine is the eldest daughter of a moderately well-to-do clergyman, and her first instruction has come from her family. Although her home is modest, her parents are well-educated and their down-to-earth manners and kind hearts are reflected in their daughter's unpretentious behavior. The senior Morlands lack flair, however, and can provide Catherine with little adventure. Living in the very small village of Fullerton, she misses the pleasures of even the most limited social activity. Because Fullerton boasts only forty families, Catherine has little chance to meet interesting young men. The narrator mockingly overstates her predicament:

There was not one lord in the neighborhood; no—not even a baronet. There was not one family among their acquaintance who had reared and supported a boy accidentally found at their door—not one young man whose origin was unknown. Her father had no ward, and the squire of the parish no children.

To fill the void Catherine reads novels. Some of them like *Sir Charles Grandison* contain moral adventures rooted in reality.

Her imagination is more readily engaged, however, by the fantastic gothic tales of Ann Radcliffe with their outlandish plots and their black-and-white character types. These unlikely tales of horror both feed and mislead her youthful mind. Catherine's eagerness and her inexperience make her expect gothic adventure when after her stay in Bath she visits Northanger Abbey. Her unrealistic anticipation stems from the name of the estate rather than its appearance. Although Henry Tilney gently mocks her romantic expectations, and she herself notices that the abbey has been thoroughly modernized, Catherine still has hopes for adventure.

Even if she is sometimes susceptible to the seductions of a fantasy world, Catherine's feet are planted firmly on the ground. While ostensibly belittling the young lady's inability to be an appropriate gothic heroine, the narrator is actually praising her steadiness and indicating her potential for growing into a thoughtful and intelligent woman. It is to her credit rather than her detriment that she leaves for Bath "with a degree of moderation and composure" instead of exhibiting "the refined susceptibilities, the tender emotions which the first separation of a heroine from her family ought always to excite."

Furthermore, she quickly realizes her mistake when her desire to see Blaize Castle with the Thorpes and her brother James allows her to assume that a previous engagement with the Tilneys has been postponed by poor weather. After the party's failure to reach the Castle results in a rescheduling of the excursion that again conflicts with the date made with the Tilneys, Catherine does not allow herself to be persuaded to change her plans a second time. Her desire for a gothic adventure in the gloomy confines of Blaize Castle is less strong than her wish to walk in the open air with the congenial Eleanor Tilney and her charming, handsome brother. Not only is the walk with the Tilneys the correct behavior for Catherine (her date with them was made first), it is also her preference. Given the choice, Catherine rationally opts for the correct and well-known over the chancy and mysterious. Probably because of her sensible upbringing, she is not a candidate for a long stay in the fantastic world of the gothic.

However, when she is at Northanger Abbey, Catherine lets her attraction for the gothic temporarily lead her astray. Partially abetted by the odd behavior of General Tilney, she decides that he has either murdered or hidden away his unhappy wife. She sets out to explore the unfortunate woman's living quarters that she had been mysteriously barred from entering during her tour of the Abbey with the general and Eleanor. Caught in the chamber by an unexpectedly returning Henry, Catherine guiltily confesses her suspicions—whose ridiculousness he quickly exposes:

What have you been judging from? Remember the country and the age in which we live. Remember that we are English, that we are Christians. Consult your own understanding, your own sense of the probable, your own observation of what is passing around you. Does our education prepare us for such atrocities? Do our laws connive them? Could they be perpetuated without being known, in a country like this, where social and literary intercourse is on such a footing, where every man is surrounded by a neighborhood of voluntary spies, and where roads and newspapers lay everything open? Dearest Miss Morland, what ideas have you been admitting?

Henry's speech to Catherine also serves as Austen's criticism of readers who are fascinated with the gothic. In her opinion, gothic horror is incompatible with English society, English temperament, and the English tendency to gossip. As escapism, gothic novels are delightful—Henry himself admits to having been unable to stop reading *The Mysteries of Udolpho* until he had finished it. However, once the gothic turns into an excuse for extravagant behavior or a stimulus of unrealistc expectation, its escapism becomes menacing and destructive.

Catherine immediately realizes her folly as Henry speaks, and she deplores her "voluntary self-created delusion," formulated by a mind that was "craving to be frightened." She calls the episode an infatuation, inadvertently suggesting a similarity between gothic romance and an ill-conceived love attachment. In its superficiality, lack of rationality, and excess, the gothic fascination does indeed resemble a romantic crush. Both stimulate the emotions and suppress the reason. It is not strange, therefore, that the man-chasing Isabella Thorpe is also a devoted reader of gothic novels. But Isabella embodies more than just the gothic excesses and superficialities. She is not simply a younger version of Mrs. Allen, an empty-headed woman who will marry and settle into an existence of adorning herself and gossiping about others. Although empty-headed, Mrs. Allen is good-hearted; Isabella, in contrast, manifests no such simplicity. She is mercenary, hypocritical, selfish, and scheming.

Like many of the persons she reads about in gothic fiction, Isabella is also dangerous, trading as she does on falsehood, antisocial behavior, and intense self-absorption. She is not superficial and vivacious by nature; her behavior is a pose. She uses language with extravagant imprecision, not because she is young and silly but because she has something to hide. When she wants to stand up and dance more than one time with James Morland, she first protests that she will not do so unless Catherine joins her. As this eventuality does not occur, she babbles that James is so importunate that she cannot resist him: "My dear creature, I am afraid I must leave you, your brother is so amazingly impatient to begin; I know you will not mind my going away, and I dare say John will be back in a moment and then you may easily find me out." To Isabella, words are not instruments of explanation, but of obfuscation.

Since Catherine takes language at face value, she is slow to comprehend Isabella's behavior. She inadvertently shows an appreciation of her friend's verbal tactics, however, when she comments on her own simplicity of speech to Henry, saying, "I cannot speak well enough to be unintelligeable." Isabella's patter is engaging and illogical, replete with attributions of villainy to all young men and wisdom to herself and Catherine. In its attachment to these oversimplified categories of good and evil, it is also related to the language of gothic romance.

General Tilney is often called the villain of *Northanger Abbey,* but he is no more evil than Isabella Thorpe. He is the one whom Catherine first suspects of villainy, albeit for the wrong reasons. He has not, as she thinks, hidden away his wife, but he has psychologically chained up his own children. And behind his disguise of solicitousness toward Catherine lurks a rapaciousness for, if not the treasures of her body, at least the treasures of her estate. Although Isabella lacks the general's authority and his stature in society, her power is no less sinister. Catherine is quite as bewildered and taken in by her friend's attentions as she is by the general's. In fact, she is more vulnerable to Isabella's appeal, for Isabella plays both heroine and narrator in the gothic tale that she has fashioned of her own life.

In order to make a successful passage into the responsible adult world, Catherine must throw off her attachment to the simplistic gothic framework of good and evil. Once Henry's rebuke has brought her back from the world of gothic fantasy, Catherine can no longer be manipulated by Isabella's poses and her seductive gothic vocabulary. The letter she writes to Catherine late in the novel trying to insinuate her way back into the good graces of the Morland family is no different in style from any of her other speeches—with its villains and victims and irrationalities. But Catherine finally sees through the "shallow artifice."

Catherine's blindness to Isabella's obvious superficiality has bothered many readers, but it is perfectly logical in the context of her strong need for a friend and confidante. Because her family and Mrs. Allen and the other denizens of Fullerton have failed to provide her with a true friend, Catherine gladly accepts Isabella's overtures. Just as her need for adventure has made her susceptible to the charms of gothic novels, her need for a friend has made her susceptible to the charms of Isabella Thorpe. In the end, Catherine is "ashamed of ever having loved" Isabella, but there is no denying that she did love her. To the outsider, Isabella appears crass and manipulative, but for the eager and unassuming Catherine, upon whom so much flattering attention is showered, Isabella provides a welcome change from her pedestrian existence.

In her letter to Eleanor Tilney near the end of the novel, Catherine demonstrates that she finally has freed herself from Isabella's influence. Both in intention and execution, the document is the antithesis of Isabella's manipulative, excessive prose. As she writes, Catherine struggles to "do justice to her sentiments and her situation, convey gratitude without servile regret, be guarded without coldness, and honest without resentment." She succeeds in writing a brief and businesslike note, returning the money that she owes Eleanor "with grateful thanks, and the thousand good wishes of a most affectionate heart." Beyond the restraint and good judgment of this letter, one can still see Catherine's need for affection and her tendency toward excess manifesting themselves. Fortunately, she has found in Eleanor a worthy and reasonable friend who will return her affection and curb her fantasies. Eleanor Tilney is the realistic embodiment of what a young Englishwoman should be; Isabella Thorpe is but the gothic caricature.

If Eleanor becomes the worthy companion Catherine lacked at the beginning of *Northanger Abbey,* her brother Henry quickly assumes the position of Catherine's guide and mentor. From the first, Catherine listens eagerly to his opinions and more than once frets over what he would think of her behavior. When she naively supposes herself on the brink of discovering an antique manuscript in a chest at Northanger Abbey and instead finds a laundry list, she immediately imagines Henry's disapproval: "Heaven forbid that Henry Tilney should ever know [this] folly!" Later when she is wiser, she still worries about his good opinion as she writes to Eleanor, seeking to compose something over which "she might not blush herself, if Henry should chance to see [it]."

Part of Henry's interest in Catherine stems from her willingnesss to be instructed. "A teachableness of disposition in a young lady is a great blessing," he says at one point, complimenting her on something she has learned from Eleanor. If Catherine is an apt pupil, Henry is a particularly worthy instructor. His manner is both wise and playful, and his language is precise. Good-naturedly but with an eye to correct, he complains about young ladies' tendencies to use words sloppily, finding particular fault with their careless use of modifiers such as *nice* and *amazingly.* He also bemoans the grammmar and punctuation used (or not used) in their letters. These observations are not lost on Catherine whose speech and prose are more guarded after his injunctions.

Because of his own mastery of language, Henry has the facility to be the ironist, the observer of style and convention, the mocker of social platitudes. In this capacity, he very much resembles the story's narrator, for they both exercise the prerogative to mock and chide. Although they both patronize Catherine's ignorance and make fun of her attraction to romance, they also maintain a proprietary interest in her. Underneath their cool sophistication, they admire her good heart and her firm sense of right and wrong. Because they appreciate her potential, the narrator and Henry feel the need to rescue Catherine from triviality and cruelty and to guide her away from the Mrs. Allens, the Isabellas, and the General Tilneys of the world.

If Henry seems to be more of an instructor than a lover in *Northanger Abbey*, it is because Catherine is not a worthy object of his love until she has cast off some of her naive simplicity. He instructs her because he wants to love her. Eleanor at one point comments that her brother behaves in the same way to both of them: "Miss Morland, he is treating you exactly as he does his sister. He is forever finding fault with me, for some incorrectness of language, and now he is taking the same liberty with you." Henry is very fond of his sister, and the fact that he takes the same kind of liberties with Catherine indicates a similar affection for her. In Austen's cosmos this kind of witty and caring instruction is not only a prelude to love but a form of love as well. It will resurface in the heroes of *Mansfield Park* and *Emma* who also endeavor to teach the women they love.

Northanger Abbey suggests that books and society provide the two major paths of instruction for unformed young women like Catherine Morland. The similar skills of the novel's hero and its narrator highlight the potential of both friendship and fiction as positive forces in Catherine's education. But the story also indicates how profoundly Catherine could have been led astray. Neither Isabella Thorpe nor the domineering General Tilney are fit instructors for her, but they both attempt to teach her their ways. The gothic novel is not her proper literary guide, either. What Catherine needs is a person like Henry and a book like *Northanger Abbey*. Both the book and the man can provide her with the combination of distancing wit and concerned good sense to turn her into a mature, well-balanced adult.

By having both Henry and the narrator discuss the virtues and pleasures of a good novel, Austen underlines that genre's educational value for a person like Catherine. Very near the beginning of *Northanger Abbey*, the narrator provides a spirited defense of the novel's usefulness, calling it "the work in which the greatest powers of the mind are displayed, in which the most thorough knowledge of human nature, the happiest delineation of its varieties, the liveliest effusions of wit and humor, are conveyed to the world in the best-chosen language." Henry agrees, although his praise is considerably blunter and more personal. "The person, be it gentleman or lady, who has not pleasure in a good novel must be intolerably stupid," he candidly opines. The obtuse John Thorpe in boasting that he never reads novels eloquently bears out Henry's testimony.

Instructive and pleasant though it is as a guidebook for its readers, *Northanger Abbey* ends rather too abruptly. Henry's proposal, the discovery of General Tilney's motives for ejecting Catherine from the abbey, and Eleanor's marriage all occur in the last ten pages. No other Jane Austen novel rushes so precipitously to its conclusion. Had she lived to further revise the work, it seems likely that Austen would have expanded it, introducing Eleanor's well-born husband at a much earlier point and including at least one scene of confrontation between Catherine and the general towards the end. As it stands, the book's conclusion appears condensed and unsatisfying.

The title *Northanger Abbey* may not have been Austen's final choice either, for it tends to give undue emphasis to that location in the story. Bath is just as important to the narrative, and Catherine greets her stay there with an enthusiasm equal to what she expresses at the prospect of visiting Northanger Abbey. When she speaks of enjoying her stay in Bath more as the days go on, Henry warns her that fashionable people always tire of Bath after six weeks. But Catherine is as incapable of becoming a fashionable person as she is of becoming a proper gothic heroine. Although she wishes her family were with her to enjoy the town, she innocently asks, "Oh! Who can ever be tired of Bath?" Henry's response compliments Catherine's openness, but it also says a great deal about Bath's other inhabitants: "Not those who bring such fresh feelings of every sort to it as you do," he says. "But papas and mammas, and brothers, and intimate friends are a good deal gone by, to most of the frequenters of Bath—and the honest relish of balls and plays, and everyday sights is past with them."

Henry sees Bath as a town for the bored and the idle, a place of crowded rooms and self-conscious gestures. In Bath there is ample space for the peevish anger of John Thorpe and the shameless coquetry of his sister but seemingly none for the finer emotions. The inhabitants are so devoid of genuine feeling that Henry finds Catherine's enthusiasm unexpectedly refreshing. The town of Bath, then, provides a kind of worldly counterpart to the fantastic settings of the gothic novels that Catherine loves to read. It is between these two realms of boredom and fascination, of pettiness and high drama that she must steer her course.

Midway between the jaded world of Bath and the gothic wonderland stands Tilney's modernized estate, Northanger Abbey. It proves to be neither haven nor prison but rather an emblem of the adult world into which Catherine has finally entered. Within it are contained the refinement, wit, and kindness of Henry and Eleanor as well as the cruelty and avarice of their father. It seems at first a place of romance, but it turns out instead to be fitted up for practical life—a life that Catherine learns will provide her with more than enough adventure.

4

Sense and Sensibility: The Need for Reserve

Sense and Sensibility is never praised enough. Because of its congruence in theme, situation, and character to Austen's acknowledged masterpiece *Pride and Prejudice, Sense and Sensibility* has suffered. The similarity in the titles and the closeness of the two books' composition and publication dates has led readers tacitly to assume that *Sense and Sensibility* is a dry run, a less polished, less subtle attempt of Austen's to tell the story of the courtship of two sisters. The coupling of the two novels is not irrational, but it is no more enlightening than a pairing of *Sense and Sensibility* with *Mansfield Park* or *Persuasion* might be. The point is not how much *Sense and Sensibility* is like the other novels, but how well it stands by itself. In fact, it is a first-rate novel, a wise and incisive look not only at sense and sensibility, but also at the character trait Austen seems to have at the time valued above all others—reserve. The story might well have been called *Reserve,* for reserve is the one quality Austen sees as necessary for survival in the claustrophobic, small-village society about which she is writing. Reserve is particularly important to women, whose dependence on the material wealth of their families or their husbands encourages them to be either overly bold or overly docile. The possession of reserve distances them and endows them with spiritual independence, or what Austen terms "self-command."

Sense and Sensibility begins undramatically, without the introduction of an intriguing major character or an interesting event. Instead, the reader is asked to digest the complicated genealogy of the Dashwood family on whose third generation the story will focus. The failure of Henry Dashwood to inherit his wealthy uncle's estate (which has been settled on the already wealthy four-year-old child of his son by a first marriage) gives the reader a foretaste of one of the book's main themes. The young child is all sensibility—a mixture of whim, charm, and temper—and the old man is enchanted by him. The patient, cheerful devotion of his nephew Henry's needy family and his reciprocal fondness for them are eclipsed by the vital insouciance of the four-year-old boy. Hence, in the first few paragraphs of *Sense and Sensibility,* one feels the power and the potential destructiveness of pure sensibility over sense.

The untimely death of Henry Dashwood one year after his elderly uncle's demise leaves Mrs. Dashwood and her three daughters even less independent, with only a modest income on which to live. How the two elder Dashwood girls, Elinor and Marianne, cope with the limitations of both love and fortune is the theme of *Sense and Sensibility.* Bound together by strong family feeling and similar romantic circumstances, Elinor and Marianne are nevertheless two widely different individuals. The narrator—and one assumes, Austen as well—prefers Elinor, who throughout the book behaves decently and admirably. Austen makes certain that Elinor's introduction to the reader is strongly positive. Although only nineteen, she possesses strength of understanding, coolness of judgment, and "an excellent heart." Nor is she lacking in sensibility. Elinor has strong feelings, but she knows how to govern them. In contrast, her sister Marianne, although sensible and clever, is too eager in everything so that her sorrows and her joys have no moderation—she is "everything but prudent." Each sister possesses both sense and sensibility, but in differing measures, and in this difference lies the conflict of the novel.

Elinor's caution leads her to say of Edward Ferrars, the man whom she loves, "I am by no means assured of his regard for me." When she discovers that Edward cannot wed her because of a foolish youthful engagement to another young woman, this caution protects her. In contrast, Marianne throws herself wholeheartedly into a relationship with her handsome neighbor, John Willoughby. When he jilts her, she suffers a good deal more than her sister does over Edward because she has shielded herself so much less. In *Sense and Sensibility* Austen demonstrates that self-command is not only admirable but also necessary to a woman if she is to remain an individual. Too much sensibility is the enemy of the independent woman, and it leaves her spiritually vulnerable and weak.

Elinor's self-command serves as more than the guardian of her independent spirit; it also informs her understanding. When surprised by Edward's secret engagement to the pretty but vulgar and fawning Lucy Steele, she has the ability to analyze the situation, to think through Edward's possible motivations, and to understand how his youthful circumstances may have influenced him. She can see the reason for his shyness and his self-restraint as he grows to love her, and at the same time she can appreciate his dutiful adherence to his earlier commitment. Rather than despising herself and Edward because of what has happened, Elinor accepts the situation and pities Edward, knowing that his engagement involves only his honor and not his affections.

In a similar way, Elinor's reserved understanding accurately assesses her sister and Willoughby's troubled relationship after his sudden coolness has caused Marianne's nervous collapse. Reflecting upon what she has seen, Elinor surmises that Willoughby once truly loved Marianne but that unknown circumstances have caused him to put his love aside. Much later, when he comes to visit the gravely ill Marianne and explain himself to Elinor, her earlier judgment is confirmed.

Even though she is a paradigm of sense and goodness who lacks the spirit and wit of such Austen heroines as Elizabeth Bennet and Emma Woodhouse, Elinor does not bore the reader. She has her own appeal, which Austen has taken care to shape. Although the society of *Sense and Sensibility* at first finds Marianne the more attractive of the two sisters because she is prettier and livelier, the reader is influenced through the author's initial descriptions to favor Elinor's quiet worth. And, as Marianne's self-centered behavior begins to irritate those around her, Elinor's appeal grows. Instead of *learning* to like Elinor, the reader is rewarded for having understood her worth early in the narrative. The "irritable refinement" of Marianne's mind begins to exasperate both Elinor and the reader at the same time when Austen al-

lows her narrator openly to belittle Marianne's self-indulgence.
The confluence of opinion between Elinor and the reader solidifies the bond between them.

In the beginning of the story Mariannne's passionate sensibility
appears attractive and sincere, rivaling the appeal of Elinor's stability and quiet restraint. However, as this excessive feeling causes
her to be rude to others and careless of her own health, it grows
considerably less appealing. In Austen's cosmos, rudeness and illness both stem from placing too much trust in the autonomy of
the spirit. By discounting the imperatives of the material world—
money, health, the society of other people—Marianne reduces
herself to a woeful state of dependence as she becomes sick and
isolated. Her carelessness of herself and of others shows neither
strength nor independence but a selfish weakness. In contrast, Elinor withstands the loss she suffers in love and independently goes
on with her life. Part of Elinor's strength stems from her sensible
acknowledgment that the world is a material as well as a spiritual arena. When the sisters discuss wealth with Edward, Marianne exclaims, "What have wealth and grandeur to do with
happiness?" Elinor replies, "Grandeur has but little . . . but
wealth has much to do with it." Still later Marianne reasserts her
faith in the power of love to conquer all: "Edward loves you," she
tells Elinor, "What-oh! what can do away with such happiness as
that?" "Many, many circumstances," her sister replies knowingly.
Such awareness helps Elinor maintain her independent reserve.

Sense and Sensibility is primarily about the value of independence and reserve, and the relationship of the two qualities. As
the novel progresses, Austen focuses on dependence as a spiritual
rather than as a merely physical condition. Mrs. Dashwood's
financial dependence on the generosity of her stepson in the
beginning of the story mirrors the emotional dependence that
Marianne develops for Willoughby a little later on. Both John
Willoughby and John Dashwood are expected to be generous, but
neither one is. Because Mrs. Dashwood has an independent spirit
and a sense of pride, she can turn her back on her stingy stepson
and move out of his house when his wife's behavior becomes too
insulting. Marianne has no such resources; she has given so much
of herself to Willoughby that she has rendered herself an emo-

tional pauper. The self-command that her mother and sister show comes from a spiritual reserve that she has chosen not to cultivate. In the end, this spiritual reserve proves to be an infinitely more valuable resource than financial reserves.

Marianne can see little value in the notion of reserve and has little appreciation of its relationship to individuality or independence. Accordingly, her idea of matrimony is the harmonious blending of two individuals into one unit. Her husband must be in every way her double. She tells her mother, "I could not be happy with a man whose taste did not in every point coincide with my own. He must enter into all my feelings; the same books, the same feelings must charm us both." Sameness, identity, oneness —these comprise Marianne's idea of love; she cannot imagine individuality in love or marriage. To her, difference is opposition. Neither can she conceive of a person who possesses both sense and sensibility; to her the two must be forever at odds. By the story's end, she has mellowed. She marries the grave but loving Colonel Brandon, a man who possesses a good measure of both sense and sensibility though he differs from her in age, taste, and temperament. Despite these differences, she grows to love him dearly.

Marianne comes to learn what Elinor and the colonel knew from the outset—that individuals are not seamless garments, but patchworks with many different and seemingly opposing qualities coexisting within one personality. The very style of Austen's prose reinforces this notion. She called her story *Sense and Sensibility,* not *Sense or Sensibility.* Her frequent pairing of such qualities— sometimes apparent opposites (reserve and warmth), sometimes apparent identities (reserve and coldness)—indicates her appreciation of the complexity of human nature. With these pairings, she is analyzing, not opposing: her use of *and* rather than *or* suggests possibility rather than limitation. Naturally, the more limited a person is, the more dependent he or she is likely to become. This spirit-robbing dependence is exactly what Austen wishes her heroines to avoid. Elinor discounts her sister's belief in "a single and constant attachment" as well as the attitude that "one's happiness [depends] entirely on any particular person." She emphatically asserts, "It is not meant, it is not fit, it is not possible that it should be so." Both Elinor and Austen believe that life offers everyone a number of options. Grand passions and perfect matches are dangerous Romantic notions.

Although in *Sense and Sensibility* the heroine marries the most appropriate person, the event does not occur until she has discovered that he is not essential to her happiness—indeed, until she has learned to appreciate other forms of happiness. The idea that life offers many possibilities is underscored in *Sense and Sensibility* through Austen's use of misperceptions. Characters in the novel continually mistake one person for another. At her home in Barton, hoping for her lover's return, Marianne mistakes the approaching figure of Edward for Willoughby. In London, when Colonel Brandon first calls, she assumes he is Willoughby. Both of the sisters mistake the hair in Edward's ring for Elinor's, when it is actually Lucy Steele's. During Marianne's illness, Elinor mistakes Willoughby's coach for her mother's and Colonel Brandon's. Some days later she thinks she sees Colonel Brandon when it is really Edward coming unexpectedly to propose to her. These repeated misreadings dramatize the human tendency to anticipate, to complete unfinished episodes. They demonstrate not only the individual's lack of control, but also his or her lack of awareness of the range of possibilities. In Austen's world, no anticipated event is inevitable or so singularly important as to eclipse other possibilities.

The plot of *Sense and Sensibility* also supports this sense of multiple possibility. For example, it is not clear until the very end whom, if anyone, the two sisters will marry. They could easily wed the two men they profess to love—Edward Ferrars and John Willoughby. But either could just as easily marry Colonel Brandon. The more one reads *Sense and Sensibility*, the more aware one becomes of how lacking in inevitability its story is. The reserved natures of Elinor, Edward, and Colonel Brandon and the secretiveness of Lucy and Willoughby make a good deal of suspense possible. Understanding that events are not easily controlled, Elinor, Edward, and Colonel Brandon—like their author—keep careful check on expressing their desires. In so doing, they also keep the reader guessing.

At several points in *Sense and Sensibility* Austen engages and then frustrates the reader's wish to push through this reserve and to understand both what has happened and what is going to happen. Willoughby's mysterious neglect of Marianne that begins with his hasty departure from Barton and continues as he refuses to seek her out in London irritates the reader almost as much as it does Marianne. His letter of explanation, which is no explanation at all, simply adds a new layer of frustration. The resolution of this mystery comes at the climax of another troubling development—Marianne's illness. Austen's dramatization of the progress of Marianne's putrid fever—the slow sinking, the hopeful visits of the doctor, the improvement, quickly followed by the alarming relapse—causes the reader to entertain the possibility of Marianne's death. With the acceptance of this possibility, Austen has brought her readers to a crisis point, too. If Marianne can die, despite the controlling influences of the doctor and her loving sister, then anything can happen. Once the reader has come to terms with all the chaotic possibilities, then Austen can proceed to tie up her plot neatly.

Marianne's recovery and Willoughby's explanation form such a satisfying climax to *Sense and Sensibility* that one might ask why Austen does not end the novel at that point. Although the two sisters have lost the men they wish to marry, they have gained strength and confidence in themselves. If Austen's theme is independence of spirit, Elinor and Marianne have achieved it, having learned that romantic love and matrimony are not crucial or even necessary for happiness. Neither Elinor nor Marianne has had the opportunity to reject an unacceptable suitor (a gesture of independence granted to all other Austen heroines), but the reader is nevertheless convinced that both would do so should that eventuality present itself. It is because they would reject an unappealing suitor and because they could live happily unmarried that Austen grants them the happiness of companionable marriages. Marriage has been put in proper perspective by the end of the book—not to be scorned (and leaving the sisters unmarried would have been tantamount to scorn) but to be valued alongside friendship and family love.

Mrs. Jennings's misconstruction of Elinor's happiness during a tête-à-tête with Colonel Brandon illustrates this point. Seeing Elinor turn radiant at something the colonel is saying, Mrs. Jennings assumes that he has proposed marriage. What he has really offered is a living to Edward Ferrars, who has been disinherited by his mother. Interestingly, the colonel's intensity of concern and Elinor's resulting happiness over the well-being of their distressed friend are not unlike the emotions the two might be expressing were the subject of their conversation a proposal of marriage. Since the two relationships are equally important, they elicit similar responses.

In a further effort to downplay the notion of the primacy of marriage, Austen does not dramatize the scene of either sister's proposal in *Sense and Sensibility*. Instead, she very quickly summarizes what has occurred. Her skill in engaging the reader's emotions as she tells her story is so masterly that the reader invariably feels some dismay at not being able to witness the moment where the heroine, who has achieved independence, wins love as well. Yet Austen knows what she is about. She is preserving the independence of her story, just as she preserved the independence of her heroines. By not dramatizing the climactic step, by keeping the climax in reserve, she keeps the reader from totally possessing the novel. So long as the climax is reserved, the events leading up to it tend to be relived—over and over again. The reader knows what has happened, but never actually sees it, thus remaining imaginatively engaged in the story, but never one with it.

Although *Sense and Sensibility* seems to be a very straightforward novel, its tone is difficult to assess. Clearly, a sense of humor is not valued in a world where those who laugh and joke the most—Mrs. Jennings, Sir John Middleton, and Mrs. Palmer—are perceived as good-natured, but vulgar and lacking in understanding. Yet the novel's narrator often speaks with an arch and cutting wit that ignores the main characters and zeroes in, often cruelly, on minor characters, who are deftly reduced to caricature. Many readers have criticized this sardonic streak in *Sense and Sensibility* as crude and consider it an immature residue of the book's first draft. Austen's satire is not a case of messy housekeeping, however. In drawing characters who are dominated by one trait and by emphasizing their shortcomings, Austen is shedding further light on her attitude toward life's complexity. The minor characters' varying degrees of failure in friendship, marriage, and family love throw the failures of the major characters into greater perspective and generate greater sympathy for them. For example, Nancy Steele's single-minded preoccupation with her "beaux" shows how superficial the process of finding a mate can be in Austen's society, if that is all one cares about. And the Palmers' oblivious incompatibility in marriage demonstrates how empty some matches actually are. In contrast, Marianne and Willoughby's involvement appears much more sympathetic, because it does contain substance. The two have several interests in common and they certainly enjoy one another's company. Their involvement lacks measure but not content. In the same way, the narrow meanness of Mrs. Ferrars and the self-absorption of the John Dashwoods in ignoring their close relatives make the kindness of Mrs. Jennings to the Dashwood girls more admirable than it might otherwise appear.

The secondary players in *Sense and Sensibility* appear less as individuals than as distortions of the solid relationships that Austen admires. They are caricatures of the qualities she thinks essential for survival in a close-knit and limited society. Through the excesses of her secondary characters, half of whom are too warm and the other half too cold, she makes clear the importance of a balance between civility and reserve. Her cold characters are clearly the more distasteful to her. Mr. Palmer's empty unsociableness, Lady Middleton's superficial propriety, the John Dashwoods' deep-rooted selfishness, and Mrs. Ferrars's meanness of spirit all stem from a lack of sensibility. They have no feelings or reactions to anyone but themselves. Their coolness is not to be confused with reserve—they are not holding back; they are simply not interested in anyone else. Austen defines the nature of reserve with the help of her secondary characters. Reserve is not to be mistaken for the lack of involvement with others that stems from coldness, meanness, pride, or want of understanding. True reserve does not evince a lack of feeling, but rather provides a necessary control upon an excess of feeling. In Elinor, Edward, and Colonel Brandon the reader finds true reserve, where a sense of honor, duty, and propriety keep strong feelings in control and protect their independence.

Those minor characters who manifest an excess of warmth are generally kinder people than their cool counterparts, but they lack an overlay of sense and are prone to silliness. Mrs. Palmer and Nancy Steele have no depth of feeling, yet they appreciate in a rudimentary way that one must get along in society. Mrs. Jennings, Mrs. Dashwood, and to a lesser extent Sir John Middleton all possess a kindness and a decency of which Austen strongly approves. Their want of discrimination impairs their judgment, but their goodness of heart makes them valuable members of any group. Their lack of reserve may be an embarrassment at a dinner party, but in a crisis it is most welcome.

To say that Austen dislikes the characters she satirizes is misleading. The two characters whom she least admires in *Sense and Sensibility,* Lucy and Willoughby, are not treated sardonically. Were she to poke fun at their shortcomings, she would diminish their dangerousness. Lucy and Willoughby are too important to be mocked. In their deceptive appeal—that selfish ability to flatter others in the interest of getting what they want for themselves—Austen provides a further argument for the necessity of reserve. The human tendency to be charmed by good looks, flattery, and good manners is demonstrated in the society's general acceptance of Lucy and Willoughby through the greater part of *Sense and Sensibility.* In each case only one person is privy to their lack of depth and decency.

Colonel Brandon's bitter experience with Willoughby is not made known until the latter has jilted Marianne. And Elinor's knowledge of Lucy's manipulativeness and her selfish insistence in holding Edward to his youthful commitment to her is painfully withheld until the story's end when Lucy drops Edward to marry his foppish but rich brother. Austen paints Lucy and Willoughby as secretive, not reserved creatures who are protecting themselves rather than others with their silence. However, she makes certain that they are complex characters—worthy adversaries—and has Elinor muse on what they might have been, had circumstances been slightly altered. She concludes that an education might have curbed Lucy's selfishness and refined her moral nature. For Willoughby, the need is discipline. Elinor sees that he has enjoyed too much "idleness, dissipation, and luxury," which have marred his natural gifts and affectionate nature.

The texture of *Sense and Sensibility,* the fact that some characters are fully modeled while others are briefly sketched caricatures, is not a function of the author's inexperience. Rather, it is a statement of her belief in the varying depths of human sensitivity and understanding. In *Sense and Sensibility* those characters who act and speak superficially do so because they are superficial. Whether society, upbringing, or a lack of natural gifts is to blame, Austen will not say. But she steadfastly refuses to subscribe to the Romantic notion of the dignity of each individual.

In fact *Sense and Sensibility* from its grandest theme to its smallest incident will concede nothing to Romantic ideology. At this point in Austen's life, Romanticism was the enemy, not the champion, of the individual—especially of the financially and sexually dependent individual woman. Her picture of Elinor after Marianne's serious illness highlights her disdain for Romanticism. In this scene, Austen mocks the Romantic idea of the confluence of Nature and temperament—the idea that internal and external weather often correspond—when she speaks of Elinor's silent and strong satisfaction at her sister's recovery while a storm rages outside: "The night was cold and stormy. The wind roared round the house, and the rain beat against the windows; but Elinor, all happiness within, regarded it not. Marianne slept through every blast." At this climactic point in the novel, both sisters are able to react to the storm of events that has troubled their lives, not with turbulent emotion, but with reserves of calm. Elinor and Marianne have triumphed—not as wild and solitary souls, but as independent social beings, women of sense and sensibility.

5

Pride and Prejudice: The Need for Society

If *Sense and Sensibility* is about learning to guard one's spirit through self-control and reserve, *Pride and Prejudice* is about learning to open up. Rather than having too little self-command and independence, many of the characters in *Pride and Prejudice*, from Elizabeth Bennet to Lady Catherine de Bourgh, have too much. They lack an appreciation of themselves as social beings. Even though they are keenly aware that they live in society, they spend a good amount of time hiding behind conventions, behind wit, and in the case of Elizabeth's father, behind closed doors. *Pride and Prejudice* illuminates the value of social interaction and social discourse, and demonstrates that society is an important proving ground for the integrity of the individual.

The novel tells the story of the Bennet family, whose five daughters must marry or face lives of poverty when their father dies and his estate reverts to his nearest male relative, a pompous young clergyman named Collins. Conveniently, the eldest Bennet daughter, Jane, falls in love with a new arrival in their neighborhood, Charles Bingley. Their romance is troubled, however, by the interference of Bingley's influential friend, Fitzwilliam Darcy, who meanwhile finds himself attracted to Jane's lively sister, Elizabeth. Because of his initial hauteur, Elizabeth dislikes Darcy and must be courted slowly. In contrast, the youngest Bennet sister, Lydia, bypasses courtship entirely and brings disgrace to her family by running off with the dashing but dishonorable George Wickham. As the author explores these three romances, she shows the important connections between friendship, family ties, and conjugal love.

At the beginning of *Pride and Prejudice* Elizabeth Bennet does not understand the value of marriage because she has an imperfect appreciation of the positive role society plays in it. She possesses sharp powers of observation and a keen mind but fancies herself independent and, in a sense, above normal social relationships. Indicating her lack of interest in marriage, she prefaces a comment to her friend Charlotte Lucas with the qualification, "Were I determined to get a rich husband, or any husband at all." Necessary though marriage may be for her material well-being, Elizabeth refuses to accept it as a given. Her subsequent rejection of proposals from Mr. Collins and Mr. Darcy underscores her independence.

Elizabeth's tendency to stand back and judge others serves to distance her from society. While her sister Jane feels bound to socialize with the Bingley sisters on account of her natural courtesy and trust, Elizabeth quickly dismisses the two snobbish women and has as little to say to them as possible. Her lack of involvement also makes it easier for Elizabeth to talk back to those social superiors who are rude or haughty with her. An unwilling object of condescension, Elizabeth spiritedly speaks her mind to both Darcy and his offensive aunt, Lady Catherine de Bourgh. Such behavior annoys the self-important Lady Catherine, but her nephew is intrigued by it.

Elizabeth is neither so thick-skinned nor so perfectly wise as she imagines herself. Fooled by the charming Mr. Wickham's attentions, and hurt when he turns them on the wealthy Miss King, Elizabeth exclaims testily to her aunt, "Stupid men are the only ones worth knowing after all." She also blushes with shame when her mother speaks indiscreetly and her sisters show off their questionable talents in public. Even her spirited refusal of Darcy's first proposal leaves her disconcerted. Once she is alone, she dissolves into tears. The tears, the blushes, and the testiness all indicate that Elizabeth's independence is less encompassing than she imagines. Reading Darcy's letter after her rejection of his offer, she realizes that she has thought "too highly" of herself, that she has put herself above society. At this point Elizabeth begins to grasp the dangers inherent in her distancing wit and her illusion of total independence.

Elizabeth's sense of her own independence is no less a refuge for her than her father's library is for him; it is a retreat from society, an attempt to be invulnerable to the wounds that society so often inflicts. But Elizabeth finds that she cannot totally remove herself from the pain of social relationships. Despite her efforts to stay aloof, she remains deeply dismayed by her friend Charlotte Lucas's marriage to Mr. Collins. Her distress over her sister Lydia's seduction and Darcy's intervention affects her even more. Finally, her growing respect for Darcy engenders a profound sense of loss over her rejection of him. Ultimately, she cannot deny being affected by the behavior of her friend, her family, and, in particular, the man who wanted to marry her.

At the beginning of *Pride and Prejudice* Darcy, like Elizabeth, considers himself above many of society's demands. While she hides her vulnerability behind outspokenness, Darcy hides his behind excessive control. Inside, however, is a well of repressed emotion, a fear of his own strong feelings, and a worry of appearing uncivil—or even worse—uncivilized. His comment to Sir William Lucas that "every savage can dance" betrays both his unwillingness to draw attention to himself and his wariness of the emotions unleased in such a high-spirited activity. He fights his attraction to Elizabeth not because she is his social inferior (although this is his immediate objection), but because he sees falling in love with her as a danger. The word *danger* appears twice in the book's first eleven chapters in connection with Darcy's feelings for Elizabeth. Later, when she chides him in front of his cousin Colonel Fitzwilliam for exposing the negative side of her character and threatens to retaliate, Darcy replies, "I am not afraid of you." The strength of his jesting protest suggests, however, that the reverse is true—that he *is* afraid of her.

Darcy's vocabulary, both in thought and in conversation, suggests his vulnerability where Elizabeth is concerned. He is capable of being wounded, opened up by her and—subconsciously at least—he knows it. In the language of his ill-fated first proposal, he inadvertently admits her power: "In vain I have struggled; it will not do," he says. Darcy sees himself as the loser of a battle and goes on speaking of his attachment to Elizabeth as a feeling that he has not been able to "conquer." As Darcy reveals emotions that "will not be repressed," the reader understands that his struggle is not with Elizabeth, but with the feeling of love that has taken possession of him. Habits of pride, shyness, and self-control have served to repress his ability to speak affectively, but his love for Elizabeth frees him—unwillingly at first—from this state.

The only way Darcy can win Elizabeth, however, is through more open (that is to say, more social) behavior. Once he demonstrates to Elizabeth that he can be a cordial host to the Gardiners, a thoughtful friend to Bingley, and the protector of the good name of both of their sisters, she finds it impossible to ignore her growing attachment to him. By the time of his second proposal, Darcy is no longer a man at war with himself. Instead, he speaks admiringly of Elizabeth's lack of repression, saying "you are too generous to trifle with me." Not only has he shifted the burden of decision from himself to her, he has also changed his perspective on the value of his strong emotions. Rather than an embarrassment to him, these emotions are now something too important with which to be trifled.

Darcy and Elizabeth learn to love one another through a number of encounters and skirmishes in the field of society instead of through a series of tête-à-têtes. Social exigencies batter but also bring out the best in them. The reader understands that had these two been left alone in a room at the beginning of *Pride and Prejudice*, they would never have gotten along—let alone fallen in love the way Jane and Bingley do. It takes conversation and action involving others to bring Elizabeth and Darcy together, and only then do they fall deeply in love.

Conversation plays an extremely important role in their relationship, for although Darcy is shy and Elizabeth witty, they frequently enter into discussions involving basic issues of behavior. They spar over such topics as the nature of humility, the value of reason and spontaneity, the demands of friendship, and the place of humor in life. This civilized wrangling becomes one of the ways they get to know and respect one another. Some conversation is necessarily small talk, the kind of filler that Elizabeth faults Darcy for not employing while they are dancing. At other times, however, conversation works to enlighten the participants and to reveal their substance. Those who cannot converse on a serious level in *Pride and Prejudice*—Mrs. Bennet, Mr. Collins, and Lady Catherine—all lack depth of character. They talk, but they do not really enter into any kind of dialogue. At the dinner given by Lady Catherine, the reader is told that "the party did not supply much conversation. . . . there was little to be done but to hear Lady Catherine talk, which she did without any intermission till coffee came in."

Real conversation presupposes a willingness to listen and to learn as well as a readiness to express one's own opinions. The fact that Elizabeth and Darcy converse so often and listen to each other's differing opinions indicates an openness in each of them that, in the beginning, neither one understands or admits. Until Darcy's second proposal, the two never converse as if they were the only people in the world; until then, their words are always spoken in a social context. This movement in their conversations mirrors the progress of their relationship. Only when they have revealed themselves and been tested in the social arena can they come to love one another privately. At the story's end, Austen shows them engaged in lengthy, intimate conversation. Withholding words as Darcy has done, and hiding behind them, which is Elizabeth's particular sin, have proved to be a kind of antisocial behavior. Regretting these shortcomings, Elizabeth suggests that both she and Darcy have "improved in civility."

With Elizabeth and Darcy's movement from isolation to civility, the reader begins to understand Austen's view that conjugal love has its roots in society. The author deepens that appreciation by showing how marriage relates to families and friendships. Although it seems logical that a person should choose a spouse as he or she would choose a friend, matters are not that simple in Jane Austen's world. To most of the characters in *Pride and Prejudice* marriage is viewed rather mechanically as the choice of a relative—a condition generated not by desire, but by duty or necessity.

Having squandered the Darcy family's good opinion and the money they gave him, Mr. Wickham needs to marry a rich woman. Hence his sudden interest in the plain but wealthy Miss King when she appears on the scene. More winningly but for essentially the same reason Colonel Fitzwilliam explains to Elizabeth that his choice of a wife must be governed by necessity. As a younger son, he is not the prime recipient of his family's fortune, and so he, too, must marry a woman of means. Even Darcy, although he possesses an immense fortune, feels constrained. He must choose a mate from the appropriate social class, someone who will not embarrass his family. For the former two, marriage is tantamount to being taken in by a rich relative; for Darcy it is an act of safeguarding the family name by adding an acceptable branch to the family tree.

At least two of the women in *Pride and Prejudice*—Mrs. Bennet and Charlotte Lucas—see marriage in the same general light as the men. Elizabeth's mother accuses her of being "undutiful" in refusing Mr. Collins, exclaiming, "I am sure I do not know who is to maintain you when your father is dead." To Mrs. Bennet a husband is a substitute for a father, and his prime function is financial support. Charlotte Lucas, who is as levelheaded as Mrs. Bennet is flighty, nevertheless shares her attitude. She accepts Mr. Collins's proposal not out of love but because marriage is "the only honorable provision for well-educated young women of small fortune, and however uncertain of giving happiness, must be their pleasantest preservative from want."

Although marriage in *Pride and Prejudice* appears to many as the safe transfer of a young lady from one family to another, friendships, too, play a part in defining the nature of the conjugal bond. There are three important friendships in the book that act as mirrors of different possibilities in marriage. Elizabeth's friendship with Charlotte Lucas seems at the outset to be solid and healthy, bound by the common interests and the common sense of the two women. Their conversation about the place of forwardness and restraint with men shows Charlotte, like Elizabeth, to be a sharp observer and a thoughtful person. However, her comment that "happiness in marriage is entirely a matter of chance" indicates that she is more of a skeptic than Elizabeth. This attitude provides the rationale for Charlotte's marriage of convenience to the pompous Mr. Collins, a move that effectively ends her close friendship with Elizabeth. To Elizabeth, Charlotte's marriage is a sacrifice of "every better feeling to worldly advantage," and because of it, her esteem for Charlotte greatly diminishes. What happens to Elizabeth and Charlotte's friendship is precisely what Charlotte has said can happen in a marriage: "If the dispositions of the parties are ever so well known to each other or ever so similar beforehand, it does not advance their felicity in the least. They always continue to grow sufficiently unlike afterwards to have their share of vexation." People like Charlotte and Elizabeth who are initially very much alike can still disagree over an important issue and grow apart. These developments are unfortunate in a friendship but considerably more destructive when they occur within the stricter confines of a marriage.

Like personality changes, worship and dominance fit more easily into friendships than into marriages. In the Bingley-Darcy friendship, Darcy, with the best intentions, dissuades his friend from pursuing his attachment to Jane Bennet. Bingley unquestioningly bows to Darcy's dominant character, assuming that his friend's strong conviction must indicate accurate perception. Pliant even when Darcy admits his mistake, Bingley is briefly angry, but never voices regret for having trusted his friend. Bingley's attachment to the man whom he has chosen as a friend mirrors what Darcy thinks his own wife's attachment to himself will be. Accordingly, when Darcy proposes to Elizabeth for the first time, he expects her to behave as his friend has and gratefully accept his offer. Elizabeth rejects Darcy's proposal, indicating that she disapproves of his high-handed attitude both toward herself and toward his friend Bingley. Upon reflection, Darcy realizes that he has behaved wrongly and works to undo his mistake. A marriage based on dominance, unlike the friendship between Bingley and Darcy, could not have been so easily adjusted. For reasons of propriety, Elizabeth would never have ventured an opinion of Darcy's treatment of a wife with the ease that she expresses her indignation about his treatment of his friend.

The most important and the most satisfying friendship in *Pride and Prejudice* is that between Jane and Elizabeth Bennet. Although they are very different individuals, and Elizabeth is clearly the stronger, neither tries to dominate the other. Each appreciates the other's strengths, while worrying about the effects of her perceived weaknesses. Elizabeth does not interfere when Bingley seems to have abandoned Jane. Even after she realizes that Darcy is responsible for the breakup, she still says nothing. Only when Darcy proposes does she indicate her disapproval of his interference in her sister and Bingley's affairs. She never suggests that he should right the wrong, nor does she try to do so herself. Throughout Jane's period of suffering, Elizabeth does little more than look on with sisterly concern. She understands the source of Jane's affliction, but does not impose her opinion or her actions on her sister. In short, she respects Jane as an individual.

Jane, in her turn, worries over Elizabeth's happiness. Told of Darcy's proposal but unaware of the depth of her sister's devotion to him, she exclaims with gentle concern, "Oh, Lizzy! do anything rather than marry without affection." Although the potential for personal change or the assertion of dominance exists in Jane and Elizabeth's friendship, the bond between them remains strong throughout the story. Their closeness does not stem from their family tie, for they are not friends with their other three sisters, although attached to them. However, the blood tie adds a level of intimacy to their friendship and suggests that the best marriages contain a dual bond.

Family ties can be reassuringly supportive, but they may be uncomfortably constricting as well. A common theme running through all of Austen's writing is the embarrassment people suffer from the behavior of their relatives. Elizabeth Bennet is mortified by her mother's and sisters' lack of breeding, and Darcy, although his emotions are much further removed from the reader's view, seems equally embarrassed by the lack of civility in his aunt, Lady Catherine de Bourgh. The closeness of the family bond renders the suffering of the individual members all the more acute. Friendships can be dissolved, but families endure. In Austen's world, a family is an extension of the self, the means by which an individual is often judged. Criticism of one's family, therefore, is particularly painful, as is the acceptance of family shortcomings. Elizabeth has no power to disown her empty-headed mother or even to change her. Her only recourse is to look to other family members whose behavior is acceptable. To her relief, the refined manners of her aunt and uncle, the Gardiners, neutralize her mother's offensiveness in Darcy's eyes.

Like family bonds, family disasters are of an altogether different magnitude than the difficulties that occur in friendships. The support that may be offered by a friend is duty for a family member. The Bennets *must* try to find Lydia and arrange her marriage after she has eloped with Wickham. As Elizabeth's friend, Darcy is under no such compulsion. One suspects, however, that his generous intervention may be motivated by his desire to become a member of her family. He volunteers his resources to the Bennets and the Gardiners as if it were his duty—behaving, in essence, as if he were Elizabeth's husband.

With the closeness and the duty that are inherent in the family bond also comes the right of exclusion. Elizabeth dismisses Lady Catherine de Bourgh's demands that she not have anything to do with Darcy saying, "I am only resolved to act in that manner which will . . . constitute my happiness, without reference to *you,* or to any person so wholly unconnected to me." She does not care about Lady Catherine's good opinion. Were Lady Catherine her own aunt, however, or were the demands those of her Aunt Gardiner, Elizabeth would not have replied so defiantly. Consideration of family opinion would have given her pause, if not changed her mind.

In *Pride and Prejudice* affection and duty bind a family together, but respect is not necessarily part of the equation. When Elizabeth says to Jane, "There are few people whom I really love, and fewer of whom I think well," she is unwittingly differentiating between strong family feeling and those feelings that are a part of close friendship. Elizabeth loves her father, but she does not respect him. In contrast, she once felt great respect for her friend Charlotte Lucas but lost both the feeling and the friendship when Charlotte chose to marry Mr. Collins. Charlotte's decision caused Elizabeth distress but not embarrassment, for Charlotte was only a friend. In contrast, Mr. Bennet's abdication of his parental responsibility affects both Elizabeth's feelings and her social position. His laxness as a father indirectly allows for Lydia's elopement, bringing disgrace upon the entire family.

Somewhere between the voluntary state of friendship and the involuntary condition of family membership lies matrimony. Austen's description of the lack of "respect, esteem, and confidence" in the Bennets' marriage indicates that she sees these qualities as necessary to a good marriage. Because they are also qualities one wishes in a friendship, the reader may be tempted to identify the two. Certainly Darcy becomes Elizabeth's friend before she understands that she wants to marry him. Furthermore, men like Darcy and Bingley who have formed loyal friendships prove in the end to be admirable spouses, while Wickham, who has no friends, is not a good husband. However, by the close of *Pride and Prejudice*, Austen has demonstrated that a good marriage goes beyond friendship and enters into the realm of family life, where duty and responsibility are primary, and emotional ties tighten the bond. Marriage is desirable in Jane Austen's novels not simply because it is a social and financial sinecure but because it is morally and emotionally the most satisfying state.

In Austen's world, the conjugal bond is social and open rather than solitary and exclusive. The emphasis on the spouse as lover becomes secondary to his or her role as good friend and well-loved relative. Because of their exclusiveness, strongly romantic or sexual passions have no place in Austen's schema. The two marriages in *Pride and Prejudice* that are based on sexual attraction—the Bennets' and the Wickhams'—are degrading to all partners. Sexual passion dies down and leaves the couples with no recourse but irony or a wilful obliviousness. Mr. Bennet makes fun of his wife, while Mr. Wickham quickly learns to ignore his. Austen clearly believes that couples who withdraw from society into some private, romantic idyll will quickly lose their their integrity.

But Austen is much too wise to do away with romance altogether. Elizabeth and Darcy's story is a romance that is fully believable. One might even call *Pride and Prejudice* a bourgeois fairy tale—a thinking person's Cinderella story. Elizabeth Bennet is every ordinary woman's fantasy of herself. Attractive but not beautiful, endowed with certain graces and talents but not unusually gifted, she is appealing without being exquisite. Yet in the end she wins everything—the prince, the castle, the wealth, the happiness, the esteem.

Darcy, too, is a figure of high romance. He is the highborn man who is much sought after, yet curiously elusive. In the end, he is brought to his knees by the seemingly ordinary, but secretly extraordinary Elizabeth Bennet. Like Elizabeth, he combines elements of the sublime with the mundane. Despite his physical attractiveness and fine character, he is socially awkward and unable to indulge in small talk. His appeal grows as he is better known, and readers easily relate to his embarrassing awkwardness in unfamiliar surroundings. Most end up forgetting his elevated status and perceive him as an extension of themselves. His appeal is carefully controlled by Austen's narrator who makes certain that he is initially described favorably as tall, dark, handsome, and rich. Thereafter, even if he appears haughty and cold, this first positive impression can never totally be dissipated. Darcy never loses his physical desirability. Furthermore, even though his positive character traits do not surface until the book is half over, his revision of his negative first impression of Elizabeth starts almost immediately. The reader never loses interest in Darcy because Darcy never loses interest in Elizabeth Bennet.

If *Pride and Prejudice* is a romantic fantasy, it is also a comedy. The reader who enters into the drama of Darcy and Elizabeth can also step back and laugh at Mr. Collins's fatuous posturing and Mrs. Bennet's oblivious chattering. The defeat of the insufferable Lady Catherine completes the circle of the reader's pleasure. Austen understood her novel's inclusive appeal and she was also aware that it might be construed as weakness. She told Cassandra in a letter, "The work is rather too light, and bright, and sparkling; it wants shade."[1] Her next three novels would provide more and more of life's darker side. As a result, they would never be as popular or as satisfying as *Pride and Prejudice.*

6

Mansfield Park:
Values below the Surface

Mansfield Park is best understood and appreciated if it is looked at as a rethinking of *Pride and Prejudice.* What Austen celebrated in the earlier book, she criticizes in the later one. The very qualities that made Elizabeth Bennet so appealing in *Pride and Prejudice*—her playful wit, her arch remarks, her candor—appear as weapons of deception in the hands of *Mansfield Park*'s self-absorbed and not wholly honest Mary Crawford. Darcy's fascination with Elizabeth's looks and lively manner is an important spur to his continued pursuit of her and to their eventual happy union in *Pride and Prejudice,* but *Mansfield Park* sees such physical attraction as misleading. The kind of social intercourse that was so important and so necessary to the development of Elizabeth and Darcy's relationship is suddenly suspect in *Mansfield Park,* where what one says matters less than what one does. *Mansfield Park* is a book about glossy surfaces and depths that are difficult to sound. It is Jane Austen's most comprehensive exploration of those deeper attractions and feelings that cannot easily be expressed.

The story centers around the growth and education of Fanny Price, who comes from a life of poverty and disorder to live with her wealthy uncle Sir Thomas Bertram's family at the country estate of Mansfield Park. Her transition is not easy, for Fanny's shyness and modesty result in her being either ignored or taken advantage of by the overly self-confident and sometimes self-important Bertrams. Only her cousin Edmund, Sir Thomas's second son, treats her with genuine kindness. The arrival of Mary and Henry Crawford on the Mansfield grounds throws Fanny further into the shadows, for they are worldly and outgoing, quickly captivating the Bertram household in a way that Fanny never can.

In *Mansfield Park,* however, the articulate and appealing characters are not the heroes but the villains. Henry and Mary Crawford, although they are witty and worldly, prove shallow, selfish, and weak as events unfold. In contrast, the sober Edmund and the extremely shy Fanny hold fast to their principles and gain happiness in the end without losing their integrity. Instead of elevating the showy qualities that Edmund disapprovingly identifies as "heroism, noise, and fashion," *Mansfield Park* explores the quiet virtues of duty, loyalty, and affection. The ministry, Edmund's chosen profession, calls for such virtues, and Fanny Price is herself the embodiment of them.

However, admirable people, and the admirable professions they choose, often lack verve. Mary Crawford speaks for many of Austen's readers when she belittles a clergyman's life and tries to dissuade Edmund from entering it, saying, "You are fit for something better." Readers feel the same way about Fanny that Mary does about the ministry: they suppose themselves fit for something better. They want Elizabeth Bennet again. Fanny is too good: she is unnervingly patient and unbendingly moral. Austen is well aware of the problem, but nevertheless sets about to change her readers' minds by pleading the case for the quiet virtues, the quiet professions, and the quiet people who will not speak for themselves.

Delightful as she is, Elizabeth Bennet needs to be reexamined by both author and reader. In truth, *she* is the one who is too good. Her flaws are minor, and her story, from a certain perspective, unrealistically romantic. In contrast to her, Fanny Price appears dull and everyday, the spiritless product of a chastened Romanticism. Fanny has considerably more than Elizabeth's nominal shortcomings: she is inarticulate and humorless, a young woman of strong moral fiber, but little social grace. She has principles, but lacks presence. What readers dislike most in Fanny is not her morality—Elizabeth Bennet is moral—but her tameness, her want of Romantic stature. They cannot easily accept the superiority of steadfast duty over passionate inclination, or the ascendancy of fraternal love over sexual attraction. But such acceptance is precisely Austen's agenda in *Mansfield Park*. She succeeds in making Fanny interesting by setting her down in an atmosphere charged with sexuality and then showing her surprising attractiveness.

Admittedly, Fanny appears the least likely creature to become involved in such a scene. But the fact that she plays a key role in the outcome of the sexual fates of so many characters adds a certain fascination to her story. Although Fanny herself appears immune to sexual attraction, she is not. What she is immune to is superficial sexuality—good looks, easy manners, flirtatious behavior. Her long-standing love for her cousin Edmund stems not from physical attraction but from their common interests and common values. It begins when she arrives at Mansfield Park at age nine and grows steadily instead of suddenly transforming into an adult sexual attachment. But it *is* a sexual attachment—one that causes Fanny pain when Mary Crawford arrives and captivates Edmund and one that later on gives her strength to resist Henry Crawford's insistent attentions.

Without any suggestion of perversion or impropriety, *Mansfield Park* assumes that fraternal love and sexual love may overlap and produce the purest and most enduring form of conjugal love. This love develops somewhat differently in Fanny and Edmund but the result is the same. From the outset, Edmund has treated Fanny with the fondness of a loving older brother. Upon her return from Portsmouth late in the book, after both of Edmund's natural sisters have disgraced themselves by eloping, he greets her as, "My Fanny—my only sister—my only comfort now." She in turn has always loved him as intensely as she loves her brother William.

When Edmund finally decides that he loves and wants to marry Fanny, his realization is described as a natural change. But for Fanny, there has been no change: her affection for Edmund has for years been both fraternal and sexual. By not articulating precisely when Fanny's attachment becomes sexual, Austen suggests the extreme closeness of the two kinds of love. Although sexual love can be rooted in superficial infatuation, as is Edmund's early love for Mary Crawford, it can also be a deepening and an extension of the kind of fraternal love that he and Fanny share.

What is suggested about sexuality and fraternal love in Fanny's devotion to Edmund is further articulated in Henry's attachment to Fanny. Once Henry appreciates the depth of Fanny's feeling for her brother William, he stops flirting and actually falls in love with her. He notes "with lively admiration, the glow of Fanny's cheek, the brightness of her eye, the deep interest, the absorbed attention" that she gives her brother as he describes his adventures at sea. The power of her feelings becomes the ultimate sexual attraction for Henry, and he longs to be the object of such fervent emotion: "It would be something to be loved by such a girl, to excite the first ardors of her young, unsophisticated mind!" To his surprise, Fanny interests him a great deal.

Austen mentions more than once that Fanny does not surrender when besieged by Henry's sexual attentions because she is fortified by her love for her cousin. Edmund, however, lacks the shield of a deeper sexual attachment and so he becomes infatuated with Mary Crawford. Unlike Henry, whose broad experience with women allows him to see a sexual appeal in the intensity of Fanny's fraternal devotion, Edmund is still relatively naive. Because of his inexperience, he is temporarily blinded by the more obvious sexual attractions of Mary Crawford's beauty and her flirtatious behavior. He must learn through painful experience the deeper appeal of Fanny's character.

Mary and Henry Crawford figure among Austen's most skillful creations. Representing the "heroism, noise, and fashion" that Edmund so looks down upon, they are nevertheless extremely engaging—even to him. The narrator repeatedly calls them "thoughtless," "careless," and "selfish," but the reader, like Edmund, has difficulty resisting their charm. Part of their appeal lies in a willing admission of their shortcomings. Henry owns that he loves to flirt and has no intention of settling down; Mary just as readily admits that she wants to marry money and that she finds religion dull. Both separately refer to their behavior as "noisy." Although they may be considered irresponsible, they cannot be accused of outright deception.

Austen also makes a point of showing in both brother and sister a susceptibility to the unusual appeal of Fanny and Edmund. It appears that Henry has actually changed his behavior once he falls in love with Fanny, especially when he visits her in Portsmouth. Even she cannot help noticing that he is "altogether improved since she had seen him . . . much more gentle, obliging and attentive to other people's feelings than he had ever been at Mansfield; she had never seen him so agreeable." Mary, too, shows promise of reform—although more randomly. At one point she kindly rescues Fanny from the persecutions of the other young people when she refuses to take part in their amateur theatricals. Later, she genuinely misses Edmund after he has gone to London, and regrets her ridicule of his chosen profession: "She was afraid she had used some strong—some contemptuous expressions in speaking of the clergy, and that should not have been. It was ill-bred—it was wrong. She wished such words unsaid with all her heart."

But the Crawfords are incapable of radical change, and at the novel's end they remain themselves, regretting what they have lost, but unable to break old habits and behave differently. The possibilities of improvement and change and the limitations of education are among the most important of *Mansfield Park*'s themes. Careful nurture and rigorous education work best on the naturally receptive and agreeable. The advantages that Fanny gains during her stay at Mansfield Park improve her immensely, but only because she is a naturally fine individual to begin with. Fanny's sister Susan will also profit from her stay at Mansfield Park that begins as the story ends, for she, too, is tractable and receptive. But Mansfield Park has done little for Lady Bertram; she is superficially more refined than her slatternly sister Mrs. Price because she is wealthier, but the two share an ingrained lassitude, a want of firmness, and a helplessness that neither advantage nor education could do much to alter.

Austen makes it clear that education, or any kind of improvement, is not without hazards. Lacking a moral underpinning, it can yield up superficially appealing products like Mary and Henry Crawford. True to his training, Henry is a great believer in surface improvement. He is especially fond of reorienting old country houses through radical changes in landscape; the more he can move around, the happier he is. His major regret over his own estate at Everingham is its being so naturally beautiful that it needs few improvements. To Henry, improving means taking control over nature—manipulating rather than working with what is already there. There is a kind of disrespect for nature in his attitude toward landscaping improvements, and a similar disrespect for people in his treatment of them. His flattering manners and bold flirtation are meant to improve Julia and Maria Bertram's happiness by reorienting them, but his manipulations are carried out at considerable cost to the young women's integrity. Unnaturally polished and agreeable, Henry's manners and his "improvements" stem from fashion rather than from moral feeling. They arise out of a selfish exercise of power, instead of a charitable desire to help.

Edmund is able to resist Henry's ambitious and ostentatious plans for the improvement of Thornton Lacey, his parsonage house, saying, "I must be satisfied with rather less ornament and beauty." To him, improvement is more regulation than decoration, a question of morals rather than of manners. In his own way, Edmund tries to improve Mary's moral stature through his arguments and his comments. He counters Henry's plans to improve Thornton Lacey by pointedly observing, with a half-look towards Mary, that "the house and premises may be made comfortable, and given the air of a gentleman's residence without any very heavy expense, and that must suffice me; and I hope may suffice all who care about me." Mary hears, but such plans will *not* suffice for her; she likes ornate houses and showy manners. To her a "gentleman's residence" presupposes an ornate facade rather than an underlying attitude. Edmund's attempt to educate Mary, to "clear" her judgment and "regulate" her notions, fails because she believes in self-interest rather than self-control.

The easiness of Henry and Mary's social behavior suggests their insincerity, the fact that they are only role-playing. Both are good actors and very much at home during the weeks of preparation for the ill-timed and ill-fated theatricals at Mansfield Park. Fittingly, Henry is said to be the best actor of the group, and he and Mary each admit that they were never happier than during this period. Fanny, in contrast, is extremely uncomfortable, observing with dismay the bitterness, jealousy, and selfishness that surface in the others as they "act." She will not take part, for she thinks that acting makes light of very real and painful feelings.

Edmund articulates other reservations when he observes that acting both encourages egotism and sets aside decorum, giving license to ordinarily unacceptable behavior. He differentiates between "real acting, good hardened real acting" done by professionals and "the raw efforts of those who have not been bred to the trade,—a set of gentlemen and ladies, who have had all the disadvantages of education and decorum to struggle through." His suggestion that his family and the Crawfords are not "hardened" actors is only partially correct. The Crawfords are indeed hardened, callous individuals who do not take seriously the emotions with which they are toying.

At first, Edmund attributes the Crawfords' blind spots to their upbringing in the house of their licentious uncle, who ignored his wife and openly kept a mistress. Although environment may have contributed something to Mary and Henry's unfeeling behavior, eventually Edmund must grant that their natures also possess an inherently corrupt core—a "perversion of mind," that makes them oblivious to their wrongdoing. Even under such an indictment, the Crawfords retain a considerable portion of Edmund's sympathy, and the reader's as well.

Mary and Henry Crawford epitomize the seductiveness of unregulated nature and art, the dangers of ease. Henry can read Shakespeare in such an appealing way that even Fanny, who has resolved to resist him, must put down her sewing and listen with rapt attention. And Mary can play the harp like the angel she clearly is not, drawing Edmund away from conversation with Fanny. The two are so "naturally" gifted at interpreting art that they are unaware of the rigor and discipline that goes into its creation. Because life is so easy for them, they see no need for the guidance of morality. An appreciation of the balance of hard work and sensitivity that goes into any serious endeavor, whether it be acting, landscaping, or writing, is foreign to them.

Both Mary and Henry need to be curbed, but because of their natural ease, they cannot believe that they, too, might benefit from "improvement." Fanny, being more naturally flawed than they, and more lacking in social advantages, understands the corrective that structure can bring to weakness. The naturally robust and skillful Mary can walk great distances without tiring and can learn horseback riding without effort. But Fanny must employ a regimen of walking and riding to build up her health. She loves to be out in the open air close to nature, but she can be neither too bold, nor stay too long or she will suffer physically. For her, such outings are a mixture of delight and discipline, where for Mary they are all pleasure.

Fanny loves nature for the harmony and sublimity that can so often be found in it, and in voicing such sentiments she sounds like one of the Romantic poets. However, she also appreciates nature's ability to reduce egotism by carrying the individual out of himself. Here she parts company with those Romantics who saw microcosms of sublime nature in themselves. Fanny garners a sense of proportion from nature, a sense of her own smallness, rather than her own importance. In fact, it is the Crawfords who more nearly embody the tenets of Romanticism in *Mansfield Park;* Mary even allows that her brother heroically "glories in his chains." With their organic beauty and ease, and their overweening self-confidence, Henry and Mary signal what Austen saw as the dangers inherent in the Romantic attitude.

The stabilizing and decidedly non-Romantic role of the Mansfield Park estate in Fanny's education is another of the novel's central motifs. Living back in Portsmouth among the disorderly and crude members of her family, Fanny rhapsodizes on Mansfield's value: "In her uncle's house there would have been a consideration of times and seasons, a regulation of subject, a propriety, an attention towards every body which there was not here." At first this tribute seeems excessive, for Mansfield Park is no paradise; it is the home of the officious Mrs. Norris, the two selfish Bertram sisters, their inert mother, and their wastrel older brother, Tom. Edmund is the only member of Mansfield society who actually treats Fanny kindly. Since she has a similar companion and friend in her older brother William at her home in Portsmouth, what—other than material comfort—has been gained that makes her think Mansfield so superior to her home? The fundamental difference between the two environments lies not in the people, nor in the amount of hardship endured, but in the amount of structure in day-to-day life.

In Portsmouth, people behave wildly, according to their lowest natural instincts, while at Mansfield they are civilized and regulated. The order of Mansfield Park does not render the life there ideal, but it allows for possibility, and for the growth of individuality. Left at Portsmouth, Fanny, Susan, and William would certainly have become either crude like their father or disorganized and disoriented like their mother. At Mansfield they have a chance to be something else. When Fanny muses on the growth of some shrubbery at the Mansfield parsonage, she could easily be describing herself there: "Every time I come into this shrubbery, I am more struck with its growth and beauty. Three years ago, this was nothing but a rough hedgerow along the upper side of the field, never thought of as any thing, or capable of becoming any thing; and now it is converted into a walk, and it would be difficult to say whether most valuable as a convenience or an ornament." Like the shrubbery she admires, Fanny has taken on character at Mansfield Park. She has grown into a useful and pleasant addition to the society there.

Mansfield Park is threatened by the theatrical production because acting undermines the prevailing order in allowing for wild, unrestrained behavior to be introduced. Although the environment at Mansfield is not stifling, it has its limits, and certain intrusions are not permitted. The Crawfords' presence there becomes, metaphorically, an attempt to "improve" Mansfield, to change its order, to modify its inhabitants. Just as Henry might want to "improve" the shrubbery that has grown into a pleasant and useful walk there, so he and his sister would also like to modify Fanny and Edmund and the life they live.

All that Mansfield Park stands for is never fully articulated. Because its true value is subtle and unobtrusive, several of the characters fail to appreciate it entirely. To Maria Bertram, it has become a place of too much constraint, a place she longs to flee, even at the cost of marrying the fatuous Mr. Rushworth. At least at Southerton, his family seat, she will be able to do as she likes. Mary Crawford sees Mansfield not as a prison, but as a treasure house, a source of wealth and social position. Upon her arrival at the Grants' parsonage house on the Mansfield grounds, she duly sets out to charm Tom Bertram, the Mansfield heir. Her unexpected preference for the relatively poor second son, Edmund, causes her considerable anxiety, for she has no desire to accommodate herself to his modest clergyman's existence. However, when Tom is rumored to be dying, leaving the way for Edmund to inherit the estate, she can scarcely hide her happiness.

Mansfield is indeed a source of wealth, but not the kind of which Mary Crawford dreams. In her letter to Fanny about Tom's health, she inadvertently differentiates between two kinds of wealth as she anticipates Edmund's impending good fortune. She begins by speaking of Tom: "Poor young man!—If he is to die, there will be *two* poor young men less in the world; and with a fearless face and bold voice would I say to any one, that wealth and consequence could fall into no hands more deserving of them." Mary lumps material and spiritual poverty together because she thinks they cannot exist independently of one another: Edmund must be considered unfortunate because he is not rich and Tom is equally unfortunate to be dying and leaving his wealth. Unlike Fanny, Mary is utterly immune to anything but the material worth of Mansfield Park. She never considers that a person might be poor, yet rich in spiritual blessings.

In fact, Mary is quite blind to any kind of activity that goes on below the surface. A most articulate and engaging talker, she is at a loss to interpret Fanny's silences. She always has something to say, while Fanny is often mute, especially when she is moved. For Fanny there are emotions of tenderness that cannot "be clothed in words." Because of her deep devotion to Edmund, she is unable to speak to him as she leaves for Portsmouth; similarly, she feels "speechless admiration" for William in his uniform and is all but inarticulate in her letter to Mary when she attempts to rebuff Henry's very unwelcome proposal of marriage. Fanny's inability to speak and her quietness become another of the novel's central themes. In her comment to Edmund that she likes to hear Mary Crawford talk because "she entertains me," she unconsciously puts speech on a trivial plane. To Fanny, words can be diverting, even distracting, but they cannot convey deep feeling.

Even more to the point, words can be agents of deception. Fanny understands right away that Mary's "lively and affectionate" letters to her are calculated to be read aloud to an admiring Edmund, who then will praise the literary skill and warmth of affection that her words eloquently convey. Fanny's censure of speech and her mental disgust at the facile uses of language serve to elevate and legitimize her own emotional silences. Although she does engage in conversation with Edmund, much of their communion is either silent or undramatized by the author. As he dances with Fanny toward the end of the evening at the ball given in William's and her honor, Edmund says, "I am worn out with civility. I have been talking incessantly all night, and with nothing to say. But with *you,* Fanny, there may be peace. You will not want to be talked to. Let us have the luxury of silence." Unlike Mary, who sees speech as a weapon to win selfish conquests, Edmund views it only as a component of civility. Speech is not necessary to the silent understanding that he and Fanny share. Fittingly, at the novel's end, when Edmund asserts his love for Fanny, she feels "a happiness which no description can reach."

Because of their deep seriousness, Fanny and Edmund are poor candidates for any authorial irony in *Mansfield Park.* Their stature in the reader's eye is extremely fragile, and it could not withstand the deflation of mockery. If Austen were to poke fun at the two cousins' unbending goodness, she would be allying herself with Mary Crawford, and joining forces with the enemy. Those readers who say that they miss Austen's wonderfully ironic wit in *Mansfield Park* have failed to understand what the novel is about. The story means to demonstrate that silence is often deeper than words and that seriousness is finally deeper than humor. A witty narrator would only undermine this theme.

What motivated Jane Austen to write a book that elevates quietness over spirit and vitality? What caused her to criticize the power of wit and words that she herself so winningly possessed? The easy answer is to look to her biography. In 1811, when she began *Mansfield Park,* Austen was thirty-five years old—not yet even a published author, for *Sense and Sensibility* was to come out in November of that year. She was clearly not going to marry, and so familial duty and fraternal love had probably become much more important to her than before. It seems possible to conclude she wrote about what she was thinking about in 1811. Probably feeling chastened for having expected too much for herself, Austen turned to a heroine who had a more admirable sense of proportion than someone like Elizabeth Bennet.

Interesting though this speculation may be, it overlooks the fact that Austen had always been and would always be interested in quiet, patient characters. They are as prevalent in her fiction as her lively, witty heroines, and may well be based on the personality of her sister Cassandra, rather than her own, supposedly disappointed, self. Elinor Dashwood, Fanny Price, Jane Fairfax, and Anne Elliot are all variations on the same reserved and patient type. Although Jane Austen's world was not a broad one, her perception of human nature was very deep, and from the first, she explored the obviously appealing human types, as well as those who were harder to appreciate.

Nobody will ever like Fanny Price better than Elizabeth Bennet; in a sense, this very human, ingrained preference is what *Mansfield Park* is all about. The reader, like most of the residents of Mansfield, sees little to become excited over in Fanny Price. In the beginning, only Edmund and Austen feel kindly toward her and appreciate her quiet virtue. As Edmund's kindness helps to educate and bring Fanny out of her shell, so does Austen's skillful narration make the reader look on her with a more kindly eye by the story's end. It is Austen's good judgment not to insist that the Mary Crawfords of the world ever totally lose their appeal, or that Edmund ever totally forgets Mary. Austen's job is not to superimpose Fanny's image over Mary's, but to hold her up as an alternative whose appeal grows stronger as time passes.

7

Emma:
The Difficulties of
Independence

Emma is unique among Austen's heroines because she is both beautiful and rich, easily able to marry, but under no compulsion to do so. In her wit and liveliness, she recalls Elizabeth Bennet, but because of her independence, she is really more like Austen's primary male characters than any of her women. Although she could never be termed masculine, Emma enjoys the autonomy usually allowed only to men in Austen's world. Like many a bachelor, she thinks that she will not, or need not marry, and hates the idea of changing her comfortable life. When she finally does marry at the novel's conclusion, she is still exercising the prerogative of a male, for she welcomes George Knightley into her own house, rather than leaving her family and taking up residence with him. *Emma* is Jane Austen's exploration of what a nineteenth-century woman's life would be like if she had the powers and privileges of a man.

Unlike most of the book's other characters, Emma Woodhouse has never known "the difficulties of dependence." With her benevolent, valetudinarian father, she lives as the mistress of the large country house of Hartfield in the town of Highbury, surrounded by loving friends and admiring neighbors. Other less fortunate residents and visitors in the town—Jane Fairfax, Mrs. Weston, Miss Bates, Frank Churchill, and Harriet Smith—lack independent wealth, and must rely in varying degrees on the whims or the kindness of others. But Emma is free, and in telling her story, Austen explores the difficulties of *independence*—those problems that life poses for a person who seemingly has everything.

Although Emma does marry at the end of the story, marriage and a loving husband are not the essentials that her otherwise perfect life has lacked. The man whom she marries, George Knightley, has been known and esteemed by her well before the novel opens; he has always been an important, if not fully appreciated, part of her life. What Emma lacks is not a lover but a mirror. Because of her charm and her position, she has had her way too often and thinks "a little too well of herself." Full of complacence and self-consequence, Emma interferes too much and appreciates too little. However, through a series of setbacks, she improves her conduct and becomes "more rational, more acquainted with herself" than before. At the story's end, her marriage is not a fulfillment, but rather a reward for her having developed a sense of proportion about her powers and her gifts.

Despite her obvious material blessings, Emma is the least admirable of Austen's heroines. She is also the most believable and sympathetic. Austen can allow her more faults, knowing full well that greater tolerance will be extended to her by the reader, on account of her charm and good looks. Embarrassingly snobbish, Emma at one point tells her friend Harriet Smith that she would not associate with her, were she to marry a farmer. "It would have grieved me to lose your acquaintance," she states, oblivious to her own pride, but "I could not have visited Mrs. Robert Martin of Abbey-Mill Farm." Besides being a snob, Emma is also a dupe of Frank Churchill and very foolish in her behavior toward him. Her overactive imagination creates a love attachment between the reserved Jane Fairfax and the new husband of Jane's good friend. Indiscreetly sharing her suspicions with Frank, Emma unwittingly provides him with a screen for his own secret engagement to Jane. He openly lies about his true feelings for Jane, and, through the freedom of his manners, suggests his preference for Emma instead. Although her vanity is flattered by Frank's attentions, Emma escapes being wounded by his deceptive behavior. She admits that although he imposed on her, he never injured her, and that she was "somehow or other safe from him."

What protects her is her good sense, the part of her that responds to Mr. Knightley's opinions and corrections. Although she has a vain spirit, she also has a serious one—a fact that Mr.

Knightley recognizes and reminds her of often, sometimes in anger and sometimes in admiration. Despite her shortcomings and the narrator's ironic jibes at her expense, Emma remains winning and sympathetic, for Austen always balances her heroine's foolishness with her kindness. If she is presumptuous in trying to manage Harriet's life, she is also pliant and understanding of her father's considerable eccentricities. Where she is jealous and overly critical of Jane Fairfax's reserve, she is also touchingly sensitive to Mr. Knightley's disapproval. She may act thoughtless and vain at certain junctures, but she is always sorry for her behavior when its ill consequences are brought to her attention. This willingness to admit and regret her errors makes her particularly appealing—and differentiates her from Mary Crawford, the Austen character to whom she is often likened.

More than any other trait, Emma's desire to matchmake solidifies her relationship with the reader, for the reader is also a matchmaker. The experience of reading any Austen novel always includes speculation about whom the heroine will finally marry. Inevitably, he is the most appropriate man, and yet, since the reader's knowledge is most of the time as limited as the heroine's, that conclusion is never obvious. In *Emma,* the reader has the fates of three young women to worry over and at different points in the story matches up each with both Frank Churchill and Mr. Knightley. At the outset, Emma calls matchmaking "the greatest amusement in the world," but by the story's conclusion, she realizes that she has taken the serious business of marriage too lightly. This is Austen's message for the reader as well; marriage is not a frivolous literary topic, but a worthy and important one, involving the deepest human emotions.

The three major matches that take place in the book have in common long, uncomfortable waiting periods during which both parties suffer insecurities and doubts over a happy outcome. Emma and Mr. Knightley, Jane Fairfax and Frank Churchill, and Harriet Smith and Robert Martin all experience jealousy and disappointment, feeling themselves vulnerable to unkind circumstance and limited by their own shortcomings. Only the match between the self-serving Mr. Elton and his "pert and familiar"

wife proceeds quickly, without major obstacles blocking the way.
But the facility of its arrangement and execution suggests its shal-
lowness— its material, rather than emotional basis.

Emma's matchmaking displays a confidence and a presumption
usually reserved for Austen's male characters. Her unquestioning
supposition that she has the power to choose a mate is a pecu-
liarly male one; Austen's women usually have only the power to
refuse. Her attempt to mold Harriet Smith in order to make her a
worthy marriage object is also a movement into the province of
Austen's male characters. Henry Tilney, Edmund Bertram, and
Mr. Knightley each try to influence the women they love and
make them better. Emma's attempts with Harriet succeed less
well than those of her male counterparts, presumably because she
is motivated more by pride than by her affection for Harriet.

Emma's freedom and the powerlessness of most women is a
constant theme in the novel. In *Emma,* Austen demonstrates that
the primary differential between men and women is not biologi-
cal, but material. Emma, with her fortune of thirty thousand
pounds, has the power and prestige of a man. She explains to
Harriet that because she is rich, she will forfeit nothing if she
chooses not to marry: "It is poverty only which makes celibacy
contemptible to a generous public! A single woman with a very
narrow income must be a ridiculous, disagreeable old maid! the
proper sport for boys and girls; but a single woman of good fortune is always respectable, and may be as sensible and pleasant as
anybody else!" Emma is well aware that Miss Bates and Jane
Fairfax's horizons are considerably narrower than her own simply because of their lack of fortune. Late in the book, she muses
on "the destiny of women," sadly contrasting Jane's lack of position in the world to the prestige of Frank's wealthy and mean-
spirited aunt. Wealth, and not talent or decency, has given one
consequence and the other nothing.

In order to make clear that wealth and not gender is the ultimate arbiter of power and prestige in her world, Austen fills
Emma with reverse sexual stereotypes to accompany the usual
ones. Emma herself is the most prominent example—the unexpectedly rich female who can rival Mr. Knightley in position and
fortune. Of course, she owes her wealth to the lack of male off-

spring in her family. Had she a brother, he would by law have inherited the major portion of their father's fortune. Other unusual reversals appear in the story to demonstrate that men, too, can experience those limitations generally expected only of women. Along with the usual females who suffer from poor health (Isabella Knightley and Jane Fairfax), Austen also creates the charmingly hypochondriac Mr. Woodhouse. And, along with the expectedly worthy but not wealthy woman (again, Jane Fairfax), there is a naturally genteel male (the farmer Robert Martin). *Emma* also boasts an unusual male homebody (John Knightley) and a somewhat less unusual male gold digger (Mr. Elton). Through these types and antitypes, Austen gently manifests her awareness of the inequities suffered by the women of her day as a result of the unfair distribution of wealth.

Of course, it is not just Emma's wealth that allows her to act with the freedom of a man. Her equally wealthy married sister Isabella is described as "passing her life with those she doted on [her husband and children], full of their merits, blind to their faults, and always innocently busy." In her sweet passivity, she provides a traditional model of "right feminine happiness," far removed from Emma's active temper that is always busy but never innocent. It is Emma's active imagination, coupled with her important position, that makes her influential and able to do mischief.

Austen does not fault Emma for having imagination; indeed, she admires vision and acute powers of observation, at least as they are manifested in people like Mr. Knightley. He is the one person in the story who has a sufficiently keen imagination to suspect the unvoiced attachment between Frank and Jane. In contrast, Emma's vision seems whimsical rather than thoughtful because she lacks Mr. Knightley's good sense and is inflated by romantic notions. Where there is little or no evidence, Emma readily gives in to romantic assumptions. Entranced with the idea that Harriet is the natural daughter of a highborn gentleman and basing this belief solely on Harriet's beauty and her adequate allowance, Emma totally disregards more potent indicators of her friend's middle-class status. Emma manufactures the romance between Jane and Mr. Dixon in the same way, using the flimsiest bits of circumstantial evidence, all the while knowing little of Jane and nothing of Dixon. Often, though, Emma's perceptions are apt and intelligent: she correctly suspects Frank Churchill of superficiality and insincerity when she first meets him, and she immediately assesses Mrs. Elton's character flaws. Although she makes a number of mistakes in judgment, hers is almost always a willful blindness. Emma believes what she wants, rather than what she sees, but her ability to see is never really in question.

Mr. Knightley observes that Emma has been "spoiled by being the cleverest of her family. At ten years old, she had the misfortune of being able to answer questions that puzzled her sister at seventeen." This cleverness, which Emma learns to channel wisely by the end of the story, has its counterpart in Austen herself. In her first novels, Austen turned her satiric wit cruelly against those types whom she disliked, revealing herself as perhaps too eager to expose her readers to the fatuousness of people like John Thorpe, the John Dashwoods, and Mrs. Bennet. Indeed, the early work often shows Austen overplaying her imaginative skills. However, after writing *Mansfield Park,* in which she questioned the uses of wit and words, Austen became as careful with her powers as the chastened Emma. Her mockery of Harriet, Miss Bates, and Emma herself is kinder than the reader would have expected from what had gone before. Instead of the one-dimensional caricatures of her earlier work, these characters seem to be human beings, upon whose flaws Austen turns a satiric eye from time to time. Even the Eltons, who are treated less kindly than the rest, are accorded some understanding for their behavior. Like Emma, Austen has realized that her position and her skill have given her the power to bully as well as to enlighten.

In her previous novels, Austen had always apportioned between her hero and her heroine the gifts of wealth, wit, and wisdom so that when the pair finally came together, they had everything. Emma, alone of her creations, has everything *before* she marries. In 1815 when Austen completed *Emma* she had three novels in print and the self-esteem that comes from a growing success. At the time, she probably would have liked to marry a man who resembled Mr. Knightley, but she did not need to. She had achieved, without resorting to marriage, considerable stature in

her own right. Without possessing all of Emma's gifts, Austen
had earned the most important one of them—an independent status. The assured and mellow tone of *Emma* reveals the author at
the height of her self-confidence.

The relationship between Emma and Mr. Knightley reflects
Austen's appreciation of her own independence. Emma is in no
way Mr. Knightley's subordinate, or even a complement to him;
she is always his equal. The two share the same physical blessings—good looks, robust good health, and enormous wealth.
Both are also supremely confident in their speech. Their conversations (even when Emma has not yet curbed her overactive romantic imagination) reveal a sharpness of intelligence and a
willingness to speak out. When she argues with Mr. Knightley,
Emma proves a worthy adversary whether the subject be a woman's right to refuse an offer of marriage, or Frank Churchill's
failure to do his duty in visiting his new stepmother. Although
her youth and lack of discipline may initially make her seem inferior to Mr. Knightley, she is not. Her intentions are always good,
and if she assesses Harriet's potential too highly in trying to or-
chestrate her marriage to Mr. Elton, Mr. Knightley has done the
opposite. When she confesses her error in judgment, Mr. Knightley reciprocates with his own admission, allowing that Emma
"would have chosen for [Elton] better than he has chosen for
himself. Harriet Smith has some first-rate qualities, which Mrs.
Elton is totally without. [She is] an unpretending, simple-minded,
artless girl—infinitely to be preferred by any man of sense and
taste to such a woman as Mrs. Elton."

Besides sharing material and spiritual independence, Emma and
Mr. Knightley have in common their strong family feeling. Both
have a great fondness for their nieces and nephews and an en-
dearing solicitude for Emma's father. That Mr. Knightley's brother
has married Emma's sister further suggests their equal standing in
the family. However, their conversation at the Crown ball plays
down the fraternal relationship, suggesting instead a sexual bond:

"Whom are you going to dance with?" asked Mr. Knightley.
She hesitated a moment, and then replied, "With you if you will ask
me."

"Will you?" said he, offering his hand.

"Indeed I will. You have shown me that you can dance, and you know that we are not really so much brother and sister as to make it at all improper."

"Brother and sister! no, indeed."

With each in turn protesting the lack of a blood tie, this exchange indicates their reciprocal, if buried, sexual attraction. The give-and-take of their conversation further suggests their equal status: Emma does not wait passively for an invitation to dance, and although Mr. Knightley finally makes the formal request, his approach is tentative, granting her an active participation in the choice.

The theme of being able to choose rather than just be chosen appears often in *Emma*, and is always accompanied by a suggestion that the compliment of being chosen obscures the recipient's true inclinations. Flattered at being singled out, a person will often invent a love where no such feeling previously existed. Mr. Weston's first marriage was less happy than his second because he was the one chosen, and in consequence he did not carefully consider the attachment. Emma, fully understanding the dynamics of being chosen in marriage, knows that Harriet will want to marry Mr. Elton simply because he has asked her. A pronounced lack of equality exists in each case: one member dispenses the affection; the other gratefully receives it. The more appealing alternative to this situation is a mutual choice that necessarily involves the doubts and fears of both parties. Here again, Austen allows Emma and Mr. Knightley an equal footing. Independently, and with "some doubt of a return" of their affections, each chooses the other as an ideal mate. Emma sees Mr. Knightley as the only person who "must" marry her, while he considers her "faultless in spite of all her faults."

Although Mr. Knightley comes across as a sensible individual, part of him is as romantic as Emma is. Austen purposely casts a romantic aura around him by giving him his suggestive name and having him reside in what was in former times an abbey. His disinclination to dance adds to his romantic stature, for he appears splendid in his isolation at the Crown ball among the husbands and fathers and whist players: "He could not have appeared to greater advantage perhaps anywhere, than where he had placed himself. His tall, firm, upright figure, among the bulky forms and stooping shoulders of the elderly men, was such as Emma felt must draw everybody's eyes."

Although Emma's Pygmalion-like attempts to mold Harriet Smith make her seem more romantic than Mr. Knightley, his dealings with Harriet are not so strongly grounded in reason as he himself might believe. With a greater sense of proportion than Emma, he understands that the decent and genteel Robert Martin is the appropriate mate for Harriet. Nevertheless, his gallant gesture of asking Harriet to dance when she has been snubbed by a vindictive Mr. Elton fixes his behavior in the realm of spontaneous emotion.

Mr. Knightley's romantic gestures, unlike Emma's, are grounded in sense and circumscribed by social obligation. His action of rescuing Harriet on the dance floor forms a contrast to Frank Churchill's more dashing (and unpremeditated) rescue of her from some overly aggressive gypsies on the road. Less outwardly romantic than Frank's action but more meaningful to Harriet, Mr. Knightley's rescue suggests the possibility and the importance of romance within the context of social norms and manners.

The modification of Emma's romantic notions and her affinity for Mr. Knightley become more meaningful to the reader once her likeness to several of the less perfect characters in the book is perceived. She herself remarks to Frank Churchill that there is "a little likeness" between the two of them, and she admits that she, too, might have derived some amusement from entering into the kind of deception that Frank practiced while at Highbury. His whimsical, romantic, and ultimately thoughtless gesture of sending Jane the pianoforte recalls Emma's careless manipulations of Harriet and Mr. Elton. Each arrangement backfires, leaving the supposed beneficiaries uncomfortable and unhappy.

Emma's likeness to Frank is part of the reason she finds him unacceptable. She prefers Mr. Knightley's romantic thoughtfulness to Frank's flashy posturing. Emma's upbringing and inexperience have made her careless and overly romantic, seemingly the opposite of the careful, sensible Mr. Knightley. Yet, her faults are those of youth and immaturity, and her preference for Mr. Knightley over Frank Churchill indicates her desire to master her weaknesses.

Mr. Knightley's romantic stature grows as the novel progresses so that he essentially meets Emma halfway. His rescue of Harriet on the dance floor, his repressed gesture of kissing Emma's hand after she has visited Miss Bates to make amends for her rudeness, his hasty departure to London owing to Frank Churchill's flirtation with Emma, and his spontaneous proposal of marriage to her reveal his strong emotional core. By the novel's end, Emma has done as much to bring out George Knightley's passion as he has done to bring out her good sense. They have not "taught" one another anything but rather elicited qualities that were dormant. When Mr. Knightley proposes to Emma, the two momentarily reverse roles: Emma sagely apologizes for "ungraciously" stopping him from speaking, while he romantically hopes to bring about an unlikely match—his own and Emma's.

In the felicity of the story's conclusion and the delicacy of Austen's irony, the reader tends to forget that the author has something important to say about money, status, and the position of women. Although Emma mocks society's preference for unmarried rich women over those who are unmarried and poor, she quite seriously observes to Harriet that "a very narrow income has a tendency to contract the mind, and sour the temper." Indeed, people without money often are less amiable than their well-off counterparts because of the strain and the lack of freedom that their relative poverty imposes upon them. More than in any of her other novels, Austen seems in *Emma* to insist that circumstance can change personality. Usually her heroines remain strong in the face of adversity and are justly rewarded. In *Emma*, although good character still brings about happy results, Austen seems more aware than she was previously of the affinity between the gifted and the dull, the fortunate and the unfortunate. She is now less apt to mock and more willing to explain people's foibles and shortcomings.

The sharpness of Emma's comment about women and wealth is blurred in the book's denouement, but never really forgotten, for

Austen has linked Emma not only to the admirable Mr. Knightley but also to two of the story's least appealing characters—Miss Bates and Mrs. Elton. Emma's loose tongue and her busybody tendencies cannot help but suggest her affinity to the former, and her bossiness, obtuseness, and love of consequence also link her to the latter. If Emma is Jane Austen's ideal, she is also potentially her nightmare. In the end, Emma has happily achieved the combination of romance and good sense; she has health, wealth, a loving spouse, independence, and self-knowledge. But the reader understands that if she had lost her wealth as Miss Bates did in her youth, she might well have ended up like Miss Bates. And if she had had less wealth and less sense to begin with, she could just as easily have become another self-important Mrs. Elton. Emma is appealingly human, not only because of her faults, but also because of Austen's suggestion that her fate was not inevitable.

8

Persuasion:
The Need for Love

Persuasion is a novel about constancy, about the persistence of love when hope is gone. Instead of the sense of possibility that marked the Dashwood girls' prospects in *Sense and Sensibility,* *Persuasion* dwells on the unique quality of one particular match and the inappropriateness of any other in comparison to it. At nineteen, Anne Elliot is forced to refuse an offer of marriage from a young sailor, Frederick Wentworth, whose initial lack of fortune makes him an objectionable choice to her cold, aristocratic family. At twenty-seven she still loves him, and because of her continuing attachment she has refused another offer of marriage from the rich and good-hearted Charles Musgrove. She is prepared to turn down a third proposal as well, this one from her wealthy and superficially charming cousin, William Elliot. Instead of working toward a proper match as Austen's novels usually do, *Persuasion* begins after a proper match has been thwarted. In this story Austen rethinks Elinor Dashwood's sage observation in *Sense and Sensibility* that no one's happiness depends entirely on one particular person. Anne Elliot's happiness does. After once having been in love with Frederick Wentworth, she has no interest in anyone else.

Captain Wentworth feels the same about Anne but is too proud to ask for her hand again after he has made his fortune at sea. *Persuasion* documents their rediscovery of one another after eight years of separation, slowly revealing the persistence of their love through the similarity of their responses, opinions, and feelings. Speaking abstractly of the kind of person he or she prizes most highly, each describes the other. Anne values "the frank, the open-hearted, the eager character beyond all others," while Captain Wentworth admits that he wants a woman of "strong mind with sweetness of manner." The two repeatedly demonstrate competence in a crisis and a willingness to take command, but they are both vulnerable, jealous, and prone to feelings of hopelessness when dealing with one another.

Besides sharing similar opinions and feelings, Anne and Captain Wentworth are also attuned to one another's needs and reactions in a way that no one else in the story is. At one point, when no one is paying any particular attention to Anne, Captain Wentworth senses her fatigue after an outing and arranges for her to ride home. In the same way, she notes his subtle anger and disapproval of her family's snobbery toward him when it is apparent to no one else. In slowly revealing their mutual knowledge of one another's character and the intensity of their feelings as they recall their past together, Austen makes a case for the persistence of their attachment and the appropriateness of their original intentions.

Nevertheless, the appropriateness of a match does not assure its inevitability. Austen's concern with the role that circumstance and chance play in determining events is even stronger in *Persuasion* than it was in *Emma*. More than once, she notes that different circumstances might have altered a given individual's character. Of Charles Musgrove, she observes, "a more equal match might greatly have improved him." Anne understands only too well the random way that circumstances validate decisions, and she allows that her being persuaded not to marry Frederick Wentworth "was, perhaps, one of those cases in which the advice is good or bad only as the event decides." This awareness that people, even people of the most determined natures, are never wholly in command of their fates comes late to Captain Wentworth. He admits to Anne, "I have been used to the gratification of believing myself to earn every blessing that I enjoyed. I have valued myself on honorable toils and just rewards. Like other great men under reverses . . . I must endeavor to subdue my mind to my fortune."

Fortune finally smiles on the couple warmly, and they master events. Having received Captain Wentworth's declaration of love in a letter, Anne worries that some misunderstanding will occur to send him away again: "her heart prophesied some mischance to damp the perfection of her felicity." But then she rationally grasps the extent of her control of the situation: "It could not be very lasting, however. Even if [Captain Wentworth] did not come to Camden-place himself, it would be in her power to send an intelligible sentence by Captain Harville."

Anne's power over events at this point comes not only from Captain Wentworth's fortunate circumstances—he is now both rich and uncommitted to any other woman—but also from her appreciation of his enduring love for her. Love's power and importance reach a new height in *Persuasion*. It is the only Austen novel where the heroine is not shown to be content and self-sufficient without love. Austen's primary female characters usually achieve a self-knowledge that leads to spiritual independence before they accept the proposals of the men they love. Of them all, only Anne is a wise and independent individual when her story opens. She already knows herself, but that is not enough. Want of love has caused her to lose both hope and her youthful bloom at the not-so-advanced age of twenty-seven.

In contrast to Anne's solitary and strained existence stands the long and happy marriage of Admiral and Mrs. Croft. Vigorous and browned by a happy life at sea, the Crofts provide one of the few examples in Austen's work of a long standing, happy marriage between equals. This example of "right marital happiness" proves that love can endure in a healthy marriage and not just when it is romantically thwarted and tested in solitude, as is the relationship of Anne and Captain Wentworth. In conversation, Sophia Croft suggests that separation and want of occupation cause love to fade in marriage. She frankly admits that when she was not able to travel to be with her husband, her feeling of isolation generated "all manner of imaginary complaints."

The ill health Sophia Croft experiences when she is separated from her husband is the equivalent of the fading of Anne Elliot's bloom to which Austen so often refers in the novel. Whenever Anne sees Captain Wentworth, his presence causes her great internal agitation and often makes her blush. These reactions are signs of his power to bring her back to full health, to reanimate her and permanently return the bloom to her cheeks. The ability of love to restore health, indeed the virtual identification of health and love, elevates it above all other forces in the world of *Persuasion*. More valuable than reserve or independence—those qualities that Austen elevated in her early novels—love has become the giver of life.

The repeated use of the word *warmth* to describe Anne and Captain Wentworth's feelings adds to the overall impression of love's life-giving power. In contrast, Anne's vain and self-centered family members are always pictured as cold and uncaring. Her cousin Mr. Elliot, who has his own secrets to hide, is also decidedly cool: "Mr. Elliot was rational, discreet, polished,—but he was not open. There was never any burst of feeling, any warmth of indignation or delight, at the evil or good of others." Reserve is no longer the highly prized quality that it was in *Sense and Sensibility*. The reader is informed that Anne "had been forced into prudence in her youth, she learned romance as she grew older—the natural sequel to an unnatural beginning." Austen seems to have progressed in a similar way. In 1816 when she was forty and in declining health, she became open to the romantic and probably valid conception of love's restorative power.

Love's importance to Anne becomes magnified because she is alone and without close friends. Although Lady Russell is called a friend, essentially she is a surrogate parent who like many of the parents of Austen's heroines is well-intentioned but deficient in understanding. Anne's isolation extends into her own family, for she has no good friend in a sister or a cousin, no one to appreciate her or to share her feelings. This condition hurts her both when she needs a confidante and when she is finally ready to marry Frederick Wentworth. Then she deeply regrets having "no family to receive and estimate him properly; nothing of respectability, of harmony, of good will to offer in return for all the worth and all the prompt welcome met her in his brothers and sisters."

Anne sees family love everywhere but in her own family. The most vivid example is the open, warmhearted Musgrove tribe whose affection and enthusiasm provide further evidence of Austen's movement away from her early adherence to coolness and reserve. Mr. and Mrs. Musgrove's generous acceptance of their children's limited talents, along with their own lack of education and manners, is neither admired nor overlooked by Anne. In the end, however, she greatly prefers their warmth and disorder to her own family's elegance and exclusiveness. In their kindness, their readiness to overlook faults, and their sometimes embarrassing openness, the Musgroves embody the essence of family love.

Anne pays tribute to the Musgroves' willing acceptance of their children's choice of mates, saying, "What a blessing to young people to be in such hands! [Mr. and Mrs. Musgrove] seem so totally free from all those ambitious feelings which have lead to so much misconduct and misery, both in young and old." Although she does not blame Lady Russell and her family for having persuaded her against an early marriage to Frederick Wentworth, Anne allies herself with the Musgroves when she asserts that she would never interfere with any young person's prospects for happiness. Better a "cheerful confidence in futurity," she thinks, than an "over-anxious caution which seems to insult exertion and distrust Providence."

The word *persuasion* is used in two senses in the novel—both in the active sense of convincing and in the more passive sense of holding an opinion. Austen's appreciation that people cannot totally control events, that Providence *will* take a hand, makes her favor the second kind of persuasion. She sees to it that those characters who are overly resolute in their actions or overly insistent in their opinions precipitate unwelcome events. Louisa Musgrove's determination to jump off the wall at Lyme leads to her serious physical injury. And the Elliots' insistence that Anne refuse Frederick Wentworth leads to her emotional injury.

Clearly, Austen does not champion passivity in *Persuasion,* but she does favor strength of opinion that is tempered by a willingness to acquiesce and to wait. In one of the book's minor incidents, Charles Hayter, who wishes to marry Henrietta Musgrove, thinks himself in danger of being supplanted by Captain Wentworth. After a short struggle, he appears to quit the field, and although the others are mystified, Anne understands that "Charles Hayter was wise." His withdrawal causes Henrietta to seek him out and declare her affection for him. Charles has been

neither passive nor overly assertive; he struggles briefly before
seeming to withdraw his bid. Like Anne, who admires his behavior, he knows both how to assert himself and how to wait.

Although Anne's and Charles Hayter's behavior is the preferred
course of action in Austen's mind, she is honest enough to demonstrate that it carries no guarantee of success. Luckily for
Charles, his withdrawal brings about an immediate reaction, but
Anne must wait eight years to become reacquainted with Frederick Wentworth, and then it is purely by chance. Because of the
unpredictable role that fortune plays in life, Austen favors neither
overly rational insistence nor overly Romantic assertiveness. Both
stances presuppose a control over events that does not exist in the
world of *Persuasion*.

Although Austen moves closer in *Persuasion* to an appreciation
of some of the tenets of Romanticism, she is still leery of its tendency toward self-indulgence. She willingly pictures Anne's Romantic reaction to the wildness of Lyme—her glow from the sea
air and her heartfelt joy in the beauty of the scenery. But she will
not condone the Romantic excesses of Captain Benwick, whose
wretchedness over the death of his fiancée Fanny Harville is fed
by a steady diet of Byron's poetry. Indeed, Anne counsels him to
read prose as a corrective, suggesting that the rational work of
the best English moralists will calm his turmoil. In the end, Benwick's Romantic devotion proves less sincere and enduring than
Anne's more reserved suffering. With shocking alacrity he forgets
both his grief and his lost love, proposing marriage to the recu-
perating Louisa Musgrove. She is a fine-hearted girl but a most
unusual choice for a suffering Romantic.

The most excessive elements of Romanticism appeal least to
Austen, and she makes a point of associating them with self-
indulgence and childishness. Louisa Musgrove's exuberant leap
off the Cobb at Lyme recalls the fall of Anne's frolicking young
nephew at the beginning of the story. After each accident it is
Anne who capably takes over, in sharp contrast to the other
women on the scene who faint and fret. There is no childishness
on her part but rather an adult effort to bring order and control
to the situation. In each case, Captain Wentworth is her second,
willing to be of assistance and admiring of her sweet and steady
usefulness.

Of course Anne, too, has taken a kind of fall—she has fallen in love and suffered from it. But hers is not a childish or self-indulgent fall. Her devotion is deep and persistent, kept painfully inside and shared with no one. Over and over, Anne's efforts to master her emotions are stressed as she renews her acquaintance with Captain Wentworth. In Anne the reader sees an openness to Romantic feeling but never an indulgence of herself in it.

Openness is a new virtue for Austen and a necessary one to the society that she pictures in *Persuasion.* The landed gentry, personified in Anne's father Sir Walter Elliot, has become ossified—spendthrift, isolated, and self-absorbed. Sir Walter's preoccupation with the past and with the preservation of appearances, along with his distaste for the new men of the navy who are elevated to wealth and prominence because of their competence, indicates his own want of substance. He has nothing to offer but "heartless elegance" and the empty shell of his snobbery.

Because she is not like her father and her sisters, Anne is routinely excluded by them and treated little better than a servant. She finds in Captain Wentworth and his friends a welcome change—a brotherly, open, friendly society. Shining through their conversation, their kindness, and their good sense is a worthiness suggesting that they are the new aristocracy. Anne herself views the Crofts, who have rented the Elliot estate, as more appropriate occupants for that aristocratic seat than her own family. She thinks to herself, "they were gone who deserved not to stay . . . Kellynch-hall had passed into better hands."

The insistence on the brotherliness and the friendliness of the navy families suggests that, as well as their being the new aristocracy, they are also the new family. Experience rather than birth binds them together, and Anne, all but ostracized from her own family, looks longingly to them for companionship. Their ready appreciation of her merits and their willing welcome add to the strength of the bond. In her previous novels, Austen had insisted that rank is not enough, that the landed gentry must also have character in order to merit respect. But only in *Persuasion* does she offer an alternative to the landed gentry. Frederick Wentworth does not come from a gentleman's family the way that all of Austen's other heroes do; instead he is a natural gentleman. In her abandonment of the hero who is the son or heir of an aristocratic family, Austen in yet another way is stepping into the camp of the Romantics.

But Austen is not totally embracing democratic idealism. Anne is still a member of the landed gentry and her marriage to Captain Wentworth will fuse the best of two classes of English society. In contrast, her cousin William Elliot's first marriage brought together two of the most objectionable elements of English society. Overly eager to regain wealth that his family had lost, the greedy and heartless Elliot married a tradesman's daughter for her money and then mistreated her. Unlike Anne, the young woman lacked the discernment to suspect her suitor's motives. The result of the union was misery and an early death for the wife and further social climbing for the widowed husband. The newly wealthy William Elliot then proceeds to use his breeding—his good manners and agreeable conversation—as a tool to achieve even greater aristocratic status in the courting of his cousin.

Anne realizes that were there no Captain Wentworth, she might well have been prevailed upon to accept her cousin's offer of marriage. Once she knows his true character, this thought chills her and conveys to the reader Austen's fears that the noble elements of the English aristocracy (embodied in Anne) were threatened through such inbreeding. In her earlier draft of what became chapters 22 and 23 of *Persuasion,* Austen has Captain Wentworth actually confront Anne (at his brother-in-law Admiral Croft's behest) to ascertain whether she is engaged to William Elliot. Unaware of Captain Wentworth's attachment to Anne, the admiral wishes only to know if he should volunteer to give up his lease on Kellynch-hall so that a new generation of Elliots might dwell there. The situation provides Anne with an opportunity to deny the rumor of her engagement to her cousin and gives Wentworth an opportunity to declare his love for her.

The episode is neither awkwardly conceived nor executed; how-ever, as written, it underlines Austen's social preoccupation with the moribund state of the aristocracy. The reader is asked to envision Kellynch-hall, symbol of the soulless landed gentry, losing the revivifying presence of its new tenant, Admiral Croft. Instead

Anne Elliot, its last warmhearted and right-living member, will spend what is sure to be an unhappy married life there, yoked to her scheming cousin, William. Fortunately, this vision does not become a reality, for Anne is able to resist marrying Mr. Elliot. As long as Captain Wentworth's open and vital presence remains on the scene, her cousin's calculating charm can never win her.

When Austen revised *Persuasion's* twenty-third chapter, she changed its focus from the social to the personal, and in doing so, she made it a document of the Romantic era. In place of the dutiful inquiry from Frederick Wentworth about Anne's marriage plans and their effect on the Admiral's living arrangements, the rewritten chapter shows him eagerly eavesdropping on a conversation between her and Captain Harville. Their discussion concerns ideas and emotions rather than practical particulars; the topic is not tenancy but constancy.

Captain Harville maintains that men's feelings are stronger and more persistent than women's, while Anne counters that women's feelings are deeper and more tender. She argues that in staying quietly confined at home, women are more often prey to their feelings while men, who go out into the world, soon are entangled in activities that eclipse their tender emotions. When Captain Harville cites the frequent theme of the fickle woman in literature, Anne replies, "Men have had every advantage of us in telling their own story. Education has been theirs in so much higher a degree; the pen has been in their hands. I will not allow books to prove anything."

The emotionally charged argument continues with each party understanding but not persuading the other. This overheard exchange precipitates Frederick Wentworth's proposal in a letter that he writes on the spot and wordlessly delivers to Anne as he leaves the house. Although he does not agree with her, he has been greatly moved by her eloquence about women's constancy and especially by the note of experience in her voice when she states that women, unlike men, love when hope is gone.

Significantly, Anne's exchange with Captain Harville is a conversation between equals and not a one-sided persuasion, a judgment handed down by a superior to his inferior. Indeed, Captain Harville's responsiveness to Anne's arguments indicates in yet another way the democratic openness of the navy men and their way of life. Having heard the discussion and been moved to propose to Anne again, Captain Wentworth also demonstrates that there is a democratic level of persuasion where one listens to both sides and then independently makes a decision.

The direct inquiry into whether Anne is to marry her cousin that spurred Captain Wentworth's proposal in the original chapter 23 has disappeared from the revised version. In the reworked chapter Anne, rather than refuting a rumor, explains her beliefs and exposes her feelings. Wentworth's response is immediate and decidedly Romantic. Unable to wait until he can be alone with her, he pours out his intimate feelings in a letter. Using the written word not to complain of woman's fickleness but to persuade Anne of his own constant love, Wentworth can be seen as a new kind of writer. He is beginning a new book, a book about Romantic love and marriage, a book that will supersede Sir Walter Elliot's tired old tome on the Baronetage that we see him reading as the novel opens. Unlike the Baronetage, that recorded so many loveless unions from the past, this new volume has a different content altogether. It is not a history of Wentworth's family; it is a history of his feelings. The revised chapter 23 does not present Captain Wentworth's marriage to Anne as a way of breathing new life into the aristocracy, but instead it ushers the novel's characters and its readers into the Romantic era. Here feeling is more important than tradition, and an individual may embark upon a new way of life.

Persuasion is Jane Austen's most intriguing novel not only because it is her last complete narrative, but also because it departs most radically from her usual variations on the theme of finding a mate. As with her other fiction, the subject of *Persuasion* is courting. However, its picture of the Crofts' happy marriage and of Anne's nearly thwarted union with Captain Wentworth may indicate that Austen had begun moving, albeit slowly, into other realms. Clearly, she had at least begun to consider relegating happy marriage to a subplot and bringing unrequited love to center stage. Had Austen lived even one more decade, her readers may well have witnessed her writing about women who steadfastly refused to marry or who found themselves married to the wrong man. She may quite easily have stepped into the territory that was soon to be held by the Brontës and George Eliot.

Despite the suggestion of harsher realities rumbling beneath the surface, in the end, *Persuasion* maintains Austen's faith in the desirability of love and marriage more strongly than ever. It seems clear that at forty the author would still have welcomed an appropriate marriage for herself, just as she welcomed one for the "older" Anne Elliot. The possibility of late marriage had been on Austen's mind for several years. In her previous novel, *Emma*, she portrayed the happy union of her heroine's thirty-five year old governess Anna Taylor to an attractive widower. Although this particular marriage is based on sincere affection, it is also a logical and practical step for both parties.

Anne Elliot's marriage to Frederick Wentworth is, in contrast, a considerably more romantic union. She has known no other men, and he, no other women. The singularity of their match, odd as it may initially seem, also suggests that Austen was moving away from happy marriages and happy endings in her novels. The very idea that there could have been no one for Anne but Captain Wentworth and that she very nearly missed marrying him, suggests that the author had begun to see a thin line between happiness and deep sadness. The more rational world of her earlier novels where a woman looked around and saw many prospects for a good life has been, if not transformed, at least modified. *Persuasion's* happy ending is not like Austen's other happy endings. Events could not have simply turned out differently—they could have turned out tragically.

9

Lady Susan, The Watsons, and Sanditon: Framing Austen's World

Three short works, two of them unfinished, mark the beginning, middle, and end of Jane Austen's writing career. In a way that her longer works could not, *Lady Susan, The Watsons,* and *Sanditon* frame and center Austen's literary accomplishment. They emphasize her roots and her originality and demonstrate her ability to push at the boundaries of the circumscribed world in which she lived. The earliest work, an untitled manuscript now referred to as *Lady Susan,* was probably written before the author was twenty years old. It tells the story in letters of a beautiful but unprincipled thirty-five-year-old widow, Lady Susan Vernon, whose aim is to yoke her daughter to a rich and silly young lord so that she herself may pursue an unfettered life of pleasure. In *Lady Susan* the reader sees Jane Austen at the beginning of her development as a writer—without irony, without subtlety, and without a moral and engaging young heroine. But the germ of the future novels is there.

Because of *Lady Susan*'s brevity and lack of complexity, one wonders whether Austen was not attempting a satire of the epistolary novel rather than seriously trying to write one. Her youthful writings show a fondness for parody: perhaps *Lady Susan* started out as a joke that the author became progressively more interested in as she continued to write. The novel's characters are the broad types appropriate to satire, but Austen does not ridicule them. She must have realized that the blunt and generalizing nature of satire was not compatible with the naturalistic fiction she was beginning to write.

Austen wants to make a statement about the possibilities and limitations of women's social behavior in *Lady Susan,* but she makes it too bluntly—everything is spelled out. People either understand perfectly or not at all. There is one stunning discovery in the story but no gradual self-knowledge. Because the plot and characters lack subtlety, none of the tension or suspense of Austen's later work is much in evidence. Lady Susan is a recognizable type, but her letters are so lacking in reserve that she is hardly believable as an individual. No one as cagey and calculating as she is would so readily explain her motivations and spell out her plans in her correspondence. Particularly ironic is the notion that a woman like Austen, who wrote such guarded and seemingly trivial letters herself, should create a group of correspondents in *Lady Susan* who are so completely lacking in reserve, so willing to say exactly what they think.

As a consequence of all the openness and analysis in the novel's letters, no room is left for readers to draw their own conclusions about Lady Susan or to admire her spirit and skill. She reveals so much negative information about herself that one has no alternative but to dislike her. By the story's end, Austen sees to it that virtually everyone has shunned her—readers and fictional characters alike. Only two people continue to admire her: Mr. Manwaring, her former lover, and Sir James Martin, the brainless young lord whom she has been unable to force upon her daughter. She marries the latter and prolongs her flirtation with the former, suggesting through her actions that anyone who remains smitten with her is either a knave or a fool.

If Lady Susan is too completely without morals and without friends, Catherine Vernon, her hostess and relative by marriage, is too completely in possession of both. Good, wise, and astute, she understands immediately that Lady Susan is a self-centered coquette and an uncaring mother. She readily perceives that the neglected daughter Frederica is not ungrateful and rebellious but a worthwhile and naturally decent individual who is terrified of her mother. No sooner has Lady Susan formed the intention of captivating Catherine's brother Reginald than Catherine can be found guessing this scheme. Says Lady Susan in a letter to her friend Mrs. Johnson, "there is exquisite pleasure in subduing an insolent spirit, in making a person pre-determined to dislike, acknowledge one's superiority. . . . This project will serve at least to amuse me." Catherine Vernon has a sterner interpretation of Lady Susan's motives, which she readily explains to her mother: "Lady Susan's intentions are of course those of absolute coquetry, or a desire of universal admiration."

Catherine's ability to understand Lady Susan and Lady Susan's similar capacity to understand and manipulate young men leaves the reader feeling strangely uneasy. Is the world so predictable? Are individuals so malleable? With no chance to interpret the text or to entertain a wavering opinion about any one of the characters, the reader becomes part of the book's pattern—just one more perfectly understood individual, a creature totally manipulated by the author.

The complete control that Austen exerts over the reader's understanding disappears when she abandons the epistolary form and introduces an ironic narrator. By breaking off the letters and allowing a first-person narrator to tie up the story's loose ends, Austen discovers the voice that will become so familiar in her later fiction: "This correspondence, by a meeting between some of the parties and a separation between others, could not, to the great detriment of the Post Office revenue, be continued longer." The introduction of the narrator has made irony possible. Feeling privy to insights that Austen's characters lack the perspective to grasp, readers see that the narrator is winking at them. When implication and insinuation enter the text, the world of *Lady Susan* becomes a more interesting and less predictable place.

Lady Susan is the only Austen work where the main character is not an upright individual. If, after making the transition from satiric spoofs to naturalistic fiction, the author had stayed with the formula of a socially unacceptable protagonist, her work might have taken on a decidedly Romantic flavor. More novels on the model of *Lady Susan* would have generated heroines who were sympathetic outcasts from society or appealing rogues— Jane Austen's versions of Frankenstein or Don Juan. But the young Austen, with her sharp eye and sharper tongue, was inherently a moralist and not a Romantic. Therefore, once people like Lady Susan become even slightly sympathetic, they must become secondary characters. Often, they develop into brilliantly conceived creatures like *Mansfield Park*'s Mary Crawford, but they never again take the spotlight.

Another quality that sets Lady Susan apart from Austen's later heroines is her age. When Reginald De Courcy writes to his sister about his desire to meet "the most accomplished coquette in England," he explains that part of his fascination stems from her ability to captivate "without the charm of youth." Austen makes very clear that it is not simply Lady Susan's beauty that makes her so irresistible; it is also her way with words. Her beauty has aged well, but her conversational skill is age-proof. Characteristically, Lady Susan speaks for herself on the issue: "If I am vain of anything, it is of my eloquence. Consideration and esteem as surely follow command of language, as admiration waits on beauty." Indeed, even the critical Catherine Vernon is impressed: the only sympathetic words Austen allows her to speak about Lady Susan refer to her skillful conversation. But Catherine also insists that Lady Susan is abusing her gifts, and she thereby introduces Austen's readers to what will become the author's lifelong ambivalence toward captivating speakers.

Whether Austen would have returned later in life to the attractive and articulate femme fatale is a difficult question to answer. Lady Susan was an object of jealousy as well as a source of fascination to the young author, who appears to have written the book as much to explain the woman as to discredit her. The "most accomplished coquette in England" is seemingly everything that Austen was not—beautiful, sophisticated, unscrupulous. Even at age twenty, the author understood that she might disapprove of Lady Susan, but she could not deny her attraction. And, insofar as Lady Susan used words to captivate people, she shared with her witty creator a common facility.

Although Emma Woodhouse is as beautiful as Lady Susan and Anne Elliot approaches her in age, no Austen heroine behaves anything like Lady Susan. As she matured, Austen was willing to deal with beauty and with losing "the charm of youth," but she was disinclined to create a thirty-five-year-old heroine who chooses to remain free or who, as Lady Susan does, marries only for convenience. Perhaps the author simply did not live long enough to come to terms with such a character; the reader suspects that Lady Susan never totally died away in Austen's imagination.

Austen made a fair copy of *Lady Susan* in 1805, indicating that she did not find the work embarrassing or incompatible with her interests at that time. But if she were considering the possibility of publication, she would not have named the work after her amoral heroine. Her aim was to expose Susan Vernon, not to celebrate her. The book's title would probably have focused on some abstract human quality from the story. *Delusion* seems a likely candidate.

If *Lady Susan* contains the germ of Austen's mature style, *The Watsons,* a short fragment written around 1804, shows that style in full flower. A person wishing to make a forgery of a Jane Austen work might well have penned *The Watsons*. It has all the typical Austen ingredients: the good-spirited and refined heroine who has no fortune; the reserved and handsome clergyman who will eventually become her husband; the rich and boorish lord whose offer of marriage she will refuse; the charming and thoughtless cad who will try to tempt her. In addition to these major characters, one recognizes the supporting cast: an officious brother and sister-in-law, another brother who is kind and hardworking, and a sister who is superficial and vain.

The novel tells the story of Emma Watson, who has been brought up by her wealthy, childless aunt and uncle. They have given her manners and an education well beyond the means of her own genteel but poor family. However, after the uncle's death, the aunt foolishly marries an Irish officer who has no use for his wife's young niece. In a kind of reversal of the Fanny Price situation in *Mansfield Park,* Emma is cast out and returns to her struggling family. Unaffected and unspoiled by what was once her good fortune, she remains surprisingly loyal and unembittered after its abrupt cessation. Upon her entry into the society at her family's home in Surrey, she impresses three eligible bachelors. There, the fragment breaks off.

Although *The Watsons* promises nothing new in plot or character, no admirer of Jane Austen can read it without wishing it had been completed. Lack of invention was certainly not what stopped the composition, for Austen had already mapped out the plot and shared it with Cassandra. According to Austen-Leigh's *Memoir*, "Mr. Watson was soon to die; and Emma to become dependent for a home on her narrow-minded sister and brother. She was to decline an offer of marriage from Lord Osborne, and much of the interest of the tale was to arise from Lady Osborne's love for Mr. Howard, and his counter affection for Emma, whom he was finally to marry."[1] Knowing what was to happen, and having guessed a good part of it, a reader is not as much over-come with curiosity as with regret at not being able to savor the complete story of the *The Watsons*.

Perhaps one finds much to admire in *The Watsons* because it is not a departure from what is expected of Austen. The story had the potential to be another *Pride and Prejudice,* but in 1805 Aus-ten's father died and her family went through an unsettled period that lasted a number of years. When she resumed novel writing in 1811, she was in no mood to write another *Pride and Prejudice.* At age thirty-five, with no novels yet in print, the story of the wise and quiet Fanny Price probably seemed more appropriate to Austen than the triumphs of the self-possessed and attractive Emma Watson.

Less predictable and initially less appealing than *The Watsons, Sanditon,* the novel Austen was working on in the year of her death, is remarkable for a number of reasons. It departs from Austen's usual pattern, wherein the main female character is a slightly older woman in each novel. *Sanditon's* heroine Charlotte Heywood is only twenty-two, and her role in the book is far from clear. She seems levelheaded and wise like Anne Elliot without having suffered any disappointments. Although she is not wealthy and comes from a large family, neither her physical comfort nor her mental capacities seem to require improvement. There is no obvious mate in view for her as the fragment ends.

Having made the acquaintance of a Mr. and Mrs. Parker when their carriage overturns near her family's house in the country village of Willingden, Charlotte is invited to travel with them to their home, which is in the newly developing seaside resort of Sanditon. Mr. Parker has a passionate, indeed an overzealous interest in Sanditon's future as a spa. The object of his visit to Willingden had been to find a doctor who might relocate in Sanditon. Although he is adamant that the town needs the services of a medical man, Mr. Parker comes away with Charlotte instead. One can speculate that she will prove to be the unofficial physician for the town's health. Furthermore, her interaction with the residents will improve both her own estate (that is, she will marry) and the town's.

Austen's distaste for the proliferation of therapeutic bathing establishments and for the overdevelopment of the English coastline is evident in *Sanditon*. Early in the story Charlotte's father speaks candidly to Mr. Parker against the development every few years of "some new place or other starting up by the sea, and growing the fashion, [bringing about] bad things for a country; sure to raise the price of provisions and make the poor good for nothing." His sober concern is later echoed by Mr. Parker's brother Sidney who attempts through ridicule to dissuade his overzealous sibling from making improvements. But neither reason nor mockery has any effect on the ebullient Mr. Parker, and the reader suspects that financial disaster is the stern punishment Austen has in mind for him.

The novel's major themes—illness and land development —are embodied in Sanditon itself, a town that is being thoughtlessly transformed and exploited to attract the sick. In all of her work, but particularly in *Sanditon*, Austen sees illness as the frequent result of an overactive and underemployed imagination. Three of Mr. Parker's siblings are hypochondriacs, manufacturing illnesses for want of something better to do. In the case of his brother Arthur, illness is used as an excuse to do nothing, while his two sisters pass their time outguessing doctors and prescribing their own medical treatments. The elder sister Susan in particular is a great busybody, arranging not only for the supposed health of her sister and brother but also for the economic health of Sanditon by trying to entice people whom she hardly knows to sojourn there.

Susan is not unlike her brother, Mr. Parker, who has taken it upon himself to play physician to the whole of England by providing another remedy—another seaside town—for the country's supposedly ailing health. Susan's personal "activity run mad" finds a counterpart in her brother's larger-scale obsession with the development of Sanditon. He has run mad, too, in trying to transform the sleepy little seaside village. Austen plainly finds both activities objectionable because they take the place of any truly useful actions and are destructive of both the individual and the countryside.

In contrast to the Parkers' unthinking and misdirected actions stands Charlotte's steady ability to analyze people and situations. Rather than immediately jumping to conclusions, she forms her opinions and continues to observe. She willingly revises her conclusions about both the rich Lady Denham and her nephew by marriage, Sir Edward Denham, as she sees more of each of them. Her originally favorable impressions moderate to such a degree that she comes to understand that the aunt is "mean" and the nephew, "downright silly."

Reflecting her ability to watch and wait—that is, her sound mental health—is her good physical health. Charlotte, rather than engage in "self-doctoring," admits that she is more comfortable listening to professional advice. She has been raised in an extremely healthy family on a country farm where there is plenty for everyone to do. Their good health comes not only from their location but also from their being too occupied to worry constantly about getting sick.

Austen is not against doctors; neither is she against builders. However, in *Sanditon* she makes clear her disdain for people who usurp an occupation for which they have no skill or who take over a place to which they have no valid claim. She seems squarely in favor of letting certain ailments run their natural course, just as she would let certain communities grow at their own pace. Illness in other Austen books, notably *Sense and Sensibility* and *Persuasion,* is an indication of a lack of self-command and a lack of independence that results from some personal failing. In *Sanditon* Austen expands the idea of illness in individuals so that it encompasses large segments of English society. Just as a person without a feeling of self-worth allows himself or herself to become ill, so a society that has lost its sense of worth and grown overly self-conscious will also become hypochondriac, building an excessive number of watering places in an effort to restore the general health.

Austen's attitude toward illness and development is clear to the reader of the *Sanditon* fragment, but a question remains. What is to be the role of Charlotte Heywood, with her very good health and very good sense? Will her fate suggest that there is hope for a physically developing and insecure England in the way that Anne Elliot's fate provided an alternative to an increasingly effete and snobbish English class system in *Persuasion*? The key seems to lie in what her relationship will be with the Parkers' attractive, ironic brother Sidney.

Sidney is mentioned several times before he actually appears, and as with most Austen heroes (Henry Tilney is the exception), he does not immediately strike the reader as an ideal mate for the heroine. In Austen's novels, it is not until the reader hears two people conversing and sees them reacting to one another that the possibility of marriage can be entertained. Neither station, nor looks, nor situation will generate love in Austen's world; only verbal chemistry and proper social behavior can form the bonds of true affection. Sidney has just met Charlotte when *Sanditon* ends and nothing has passed between them more than his "very well-bred bow and proper address to Miss Heywood on her being named to him."

Indeed, on first impression Sidney seems the likely candidate for Charlotte's husband only because there is no one else in view. However, once the reader accepts the notion, they become a fascinating pair. Mr. Parker refers to Sidney as one who

pretends to laugh at my improvements. Sidney says anything you know. He has always said what he chose of and to us all. . . . There is someone in most families privileged by superior abilities or spirits to say anything. In ours, it is Sidney, who is a very clever young man, and with great powers of pleasing. He lives too much in the world to be settled; that is his only fault.

In this description, one is struck by Sidney's resemblance to Emma Woodhouse. The cleverness, the high spirits, the unwillingness to settle down—all these traits are Emma's, too. And Charlotte, in her turn, resembles the wise but appealing Mr. Knightley. In *Emma*, Austen placed her heroine in the situation of a man; in *Sanditon* she endows her heroine with the disposition of a man. This reversal, the cool and confident heroine paired with a witty and irreverent hero, is most intriguing, and upon reflection, not totally unexpected. The reader can see the germ of it in *Persuasion* where Thomas Wentworth is more open, more lacking in reserve than any of the four heroes who precede him.

Of all Austen's heroes, only Henry Tilney in *Northanger Abbey* manifests Sidney Parker's wit and good breeding. But since Charlotte Heywood is more intellectually sophisticated than the seventeen-year-old Catherine Morland, the interplay between her and Sidney is bound to be different. Henry teases Catherine about her interest in gothic fiction for the reason that it sometimes gets the better of her judgment. Sidney, on the other hand, makes a joke of his family's hypochondria, suggesting that his brother turn his old house into a hospital for their sickly siblings. Where Henry jibes at literary excesses, Sidney aims at social excesses. His focus is broader than Henry's, calling attention to both his family's and his country's fixation with health. Whether he would have chided Charlotte for some soon-to-be-revealed foible is anyone's guess. He certainly would not have mocked her attitude toward health, for she is the natural embodiment of everything he esteems.

The parallelism between *Sanditon* and *Northanger Abbey* extends far beyond the similarities of the two heroes. *Northanger Abbey* had not been published when Austen began *Sanditon,* but references in the text and in a letter indicate that she had recently been revising it. There is a strong sense that the later work was to be a kind of companion piece. In each novel a naive character mistakenly believes that a certain place is imbued with magical possibilities. Catherine Morland's misjudgment of Northanger Abbey stems from her overly rich diet of gothic novels. Mr. Parker's dream of transforming the village of Sanditon into another Bath or Brighton is born out of a naive faith that development is the best treatment for an England that finds itself strangely at peace after many years of war.

The real menace in both books, however, is not innocent excess but crass materialism. General Tilney shows kindness to Catherine only as long as he believes she is an heiress; when he discovers that she has no money, he cruelly ejects her from his house. One suspects that the manipulative Lady Denham, who married her first husband for his money and her second for his title, is out to exploit her business partner Mr. Parker and the town of Sanditon in the same way. She seems more motivated by heartless greed than by naive vision, and one suspects that if her schemes fail, she will quickly abandon both her partner and his town. In *Northanger Abbey* Austen feared the grasping aristocracy; in *Sanditon* her concern has turned to the social-climbing middle class.

Sir Edward Denham's attachment to the language and sentiment of Romantic poetry in *Sanditon* recalls Isabella Thorpe's adoration of the gothic in *Northanger Abbey*. Yet they are both rational, scheming pragmatists—fortune hunters who manipulate emotion and use the language they profess to love with cold calculation. As Isabella misleads and injures both James and Catherine Morland, one suspects that Sir Edward will do the same to Lady Denham's pretty but penniless companion, Clara Brereton, who is in love with him. Both Isabella and Sir Edward characterize themselves as slaves to their emotions, but the reverse is true. The ease with which they abuse sentiment underlines Austen's persistent mistrust of any philosophy where feeling holds sway over reason.

Ironically, Austen's book about the exploitation of illness was written when the author herself was fatally ill. Perhaps her condition generated a heightened awareness of the social aspects of hypochrondria, as well as her sense of the profound distance between the private suffering of true illness and the desire to flaunt imagined illness in society. These insights, however, were not new to the author. She had always hated the society of Bath where superficial illness mixed easily with superficial society. She chose to set a good part of *Northanger Abbey* in Bath because it was a town of illusion and excess, a more truly gothic place than the Tilneys' abbey home. In *Sanditon* Austen is combating commercial excess rather than gothic excess. She is highlighting an unrealistic view of real estate rather than an unrealistic attitude toward a country estate. The problem in *Sanditon* is not only broader, it is also deeper, for Austen understood that what was being exploited in the building of resorts like Sanditon was not the desire for love and adventure, but the fear of death.

Sanditon's vision is considerably bleaker than that of its predecessors because the story ventures not into a world of fantasy but into a world of fears bred by idleness. Inevitably, Austen would have imposed her familiar structure onto the story, causing Charlotte and Sidney to save the sick land through the union of their humor and good sense. Nevertheless, the unfinished story remains disconcerting, and this unsettling impression is compounded by another bleak vision—one of Jane Austen herself, trying not to be idle, working on *Sanditon* with humor and good sense, dealing with, rather than denying her impending death.

10

Family and Fiction II: Juvenilia and Letters

Although Jane Austen wrote fiction during most of her adult life, she was not self-consciously literary. Her writing talent did not suffuse her life and inform everything she did. Essentially, she was two people, an author and a family member, and she kept those identities quite separate. What Austen wrote for private consumption—her juvenile compositions and then her letters—underscores this dual identity. In the former, she is precocious, bursting with intelligence and humor, an imaginative writer about to take flight. In the latter, she is earthbound and mundane, a cog in the Austen family wheel. The essential Austen themes are recognizable in both sets of documents, but where the imagination plays freely in the juvenilia, it is checked until almost the end of the author's correspondence.

Austen's juvenile writings begin about 1790 when she was only fourteen and continue until 1793. This dating is derived not from the maturity of the style but from Austen's having gathered these early writings into three quarto notebooks, which she called simply *Volume the First, Volume the Second,* and *Volume the Third.* The audience for this work was her family, to whom most of the pieces are dedicated. Many of the entries are good-natured mockeries of sentimental or picaresque novels, structured in either very short chapters or very short letters. A good number of them are unfinished.

Although the entries in the three volumes are not strictly chronological, most of the short farcical pieces in *Volume the First* were written earlier and are stylistically less mature than the longer, more serious fragments in *Volume the Third*. Taking broad swipes at the conventions and clichés of sentimental fiction, they are replete with unexpected deaths, chance meetings, impromptu journeys, instant friendships, and excessive cruelties, all of which the young Austen takes care to overdo wildly. *Love and Freindship* (the misspelling persists throughout the juvenilia) is a typical Austen spoof, written in 1790 when the author was not yet fifteen. Its narrator, an older woman named Laura, recounts the string of unlikely adventures that have made up her life. Her family history sets the tone: "My Father was a native of Ireland and an inhabitant of Wales; my Mother was the natural Daughter of a Scotch peer by an Italian Opera-girl—I was born in Spain and received my education at a Convent in France." The tale continues, a grab bag of exotic fact and unlikely adventure. At one point, Laura unexpectedly recognizes her grandfather, whom she has never met. Her friend Sophia enters the room, only to be acknowledged as another long-lost granddaughter. From another door, a beautiful young man appears:

On perceiving him Lord St. Clair started and retreating back a few paces, with uplifted Hands, said, "Another Grand-child! What unexpected Happiness is this! to discover in the space of 3 minutes, as many of my Descendants!

The scene is not over until a fourth long-lost grandchild enters—now, not so unexpectedly—from behind yet another door.

Exaggerated though the action is in many of the early pieces, the style is remarkably lucid. The characters may be tippling claret or engaged in ridiculously protracted exchanges over who might be at the door, but the author's command of the language is formidable. Between jokes, the reader easily forgets Austen's youth and inexperience. The very short piece called "Henry and Eliza" starts with a seemingly straightforward description:

As Sir George and Lady Harcourt were superintending the Labours of their Haymakers, rewarding the industry of some by smiles of approbation, & punishing the idleness of others, by a cudgel, they perceived lying closely concealed beneath the thick foliage of a Haycock, a beautifull little Girl not more than three months old.

Without the humorous inclusion of the cudgel, the paragraph might be the opening of any number of eighteenth-century sentimental novels.

What Austen mocks in her juvenile writings is generally what she avoids in her adult fiction. Overloaded plots, cavalier attitudes paid to parental authority, carelessness about money matters, excessive emphasis on good looks, and numerous changes of location are conspicuously absent from her published works. Indeed, she embraces their opposites, concentrating on limited plots and settings and taking a hard look at material necessity and moral duty. In her juvenile writings, Austen's humor is directed primarily against unrealistic literary conventions. As she matures, her mockery settles onto social pretensions. She becomes less interested in how other authors express themselves and more attuned to how the people around her behave.

In contrast to the spoofs, five short pieces in the "Collection of Letters" placed at the end of *Volume the Second* appear to be serious exercises in fiction writing. They sketch with surprising mastery those situations that will become familiar in Austen's novels: a young girl's entry into society; a shallow, attractive young man's attentions to an innocent girl; an inquisitive woman's insistent questioning of a reserved newcomer; a rich acquaintance's abuse of a young lady of modest means. Much of the writing in these letters is equal to what appears in Austen's published novels. In "Letter the Third From a Young Lady in distressed Circumstances to her freind," the polite young Maria Williams recounts a one-sided conversation with her rich neighbor, the condescending Lady Greville:

"Why I think Miss Maria you are not quite so smart as you were last night— But I did not come to examine your dress, but to tell you that you may dine with us the day after tomorrow— Not tomorrow, remember, do not come tomorrow, for we expect Lord and Lady Clermont and Sir Thomas Stanley's family— There will be no occasion for your being very fine for I shan't send the Carriage— If it rains you may take an umbrella—" I could hardly help laughing at hearing her give me leave to keep myself dry—[says Maria] "And pray remember to be on time, for I shan't wait—I hate my Victuals over-done— But you need not come before the time."

Different incarnations of Lady Greville make several appearances in Austen's later fiction.

There is no major theme from Austen's novels that is not touched on in her juvenile writings. Although the dilemma of marrying an objectionable individual is humorously treated in "The Three Sisters," the author's sense of the situation's complexity already gives the reader pause. Even as Austen mocks Mary Stanhope's foolish wish to marry before her two younger sisters and to receive the attention due a bride, she captures the claustrophobic atmosphere of Mary's limited world. The undecided young girl writes to a friend about the offer of marriage she has received from the unappealing Mr. Watts:

I know the Duttons will envy me & I shall be able to chaperone Sophy and Georgianna to all the Winter Balls. But then what will be the use of that when very likely he won't let me go myself, for I know he hates dancing & what he hates himself he has no idea of any other person's liking; & besides he talks a great deal of women's always staying at home & such stuff. I beleive I shan't have him; I would refuse him at once if I were certain that neither of my sisters would accept him, & that if they did not, he would not offer to the Duttons.

Two seemingly atypical inclusions appear in Austen's juvenile writings along with the more expected material. The first is a kind of fairy tale called "Evelyn," singular among Austen's works because the principal character is a man. Arriving in the strikingly beautiful town of Evelyn, the story's hero, Mr. Gower, expresses a wish to become a resident. His reception quite outdoes his expectations; he no sooner asks for a house, a fortune, and a wife than they are his. The townspeople accede to his every wish. Like all fairy tales, this one is potentially farcical and could have been made immensely funny by the young Austen, but she chose to tell it in a relatively straightforward manner. The message of the piece is clear: a man's life is a fairy tale; Mr. Gower needs only ask to be satisfied in his desires. He may suffer a little—his wife pines away for him when he is away for a very short time—but more happiness is in store. A second wife and a new life await him in the same perfect town. Nowhere in her fiction does Austen allow a heroine so many rewards for so little pain.

The other atypical inclusion in the juvenilia, Austen's "History of England," like "Evelyn," affords the reader an unusual insight into the young author's mind. According to its author, the purpose of this flagrantly impressionistic and undocumented history is, "to prove the innocence of the Queen of Scotland . . . and to abuse Elizabeth." Forgiving Mary's youthful imprudences and admiring her fortitude through her long imprisonment, the young Austen praises the powerless Catholic captive at the expense of her strong and politically astute cousin. No doubt she saw in the Scottish queen's confinement a reflection of her own limited world. Neither Mary's religion nor her threat to the political stability of England means as much to Austen as the young queen's personal tragedy. Her treatment of Mary becomes a preview of her novels, where politics and religion count for little in the personal dramas of admirable but powerless young women.

The skill and wit of Austen's juvenile writings seem to foretell the works of genius that are to come. In contrast, the letters, which were written during the same years as the novels, bear little resemblance to the author's brilliant fiction. One recognizes Jane Austen in her correspondence, but she seems entirely ordinary. Critics and biographers have always apologized for the quality of Austen's letter writing. Her nephew James Edward Austen-Leigh was the first to warn the reader "not to expect too much from [the letters]. . . . The style is always clear, and generally animated, while a vein of humor continually gleams through the whole; but the materials may be thought inferior to the execution, for they treat only of the details of domestic life. There is in them no notice of politics or public events; scarcely any discussion on literature, or other subjects of general interest."[1] Forty-five years later, William and Richard Arthur Austen-Leigh expanded the apology, noting the letters were incomplete. They reminded the reader that "a good deal of [the] correspondence is missing. Some of it is probably lost by accident; a great deal was probably destroyed by

Cassandra of set purpose."[2] Therefore, readers are not to be disappointed by the mundane quality of the correspondence: "We must take the letters as they are, without expecting to find any expression of views on such important subjects as religion, politics, or literature—subjects which might be better discussed in conversation with Cassandra."[3]

The presupposition is that Austen may seem a trivial and ordinary woman in the existing letters, but that she exhibited entirely different qualities in personal conversation and in those letters that Cassandra lost or destroyed. There is no reason to believe, however, as the Austen-Leighs suggest, that she talked philosophically about art and literature to Cassandra. She had ample opportunity in the existing letters to fill the sheets with thought, rather than with apologies for her brevity or dullness, but she chose otherwise. The knowledge that Cassandra destroyed letters may lead the reader to assume that the contents were in some way sensational or startling, but Austen's restraint in her writings was a personality trait, not a pose or a strategy that she could easily abandon. Virtually all of her correspondence is distanced—either through wit, politeness, or everyday observation. She speaks about what has happened and what she has observed, but rarely about what she has felt. Emotions in the letters are almost always conventional responses—worry over the ailing, fatigue after a long journey, joy at seeing family members. What never appears is anger, despair, or euphoria. The destroyed letters may contain some interesting information that would aid biographers, but the chances of their producing a glimpse of Jane Austen with her guard down is most unlikely. Although the author lived and wrote during the early years of the Romantic period, her letters belong to the eighteenth century in their reserve and restraint, as well as in their flashes of cruel wit. No emotional effusions or self-absorbed musings appear in Jane Austen's correspondence.

Furthermore, what Austen's well-meaning relatives and admirers have led readers to accept—that her letters are a disappointment—is not wholly true. In a certain sense, they provide a source of illumination, for they are the raw material of Austen's books. They are the novels without the brilliant ordering, without the drama, without the meaning. The reader who expects letters to gloss books will be disappointed that these documents explain neither the themes nor the impetus behind Austen's novels. Instead, the books explain the letters. Without the wisdom of her novels, Austen's letters are trite and meaningless; but with the novels as an amplifier, the letters highlight the dilemma of an educated, unmarried woman of little fortune in early nineteenth-century England.

The subject of the letters, like the subject of the novels, is society. The visits, the balls, the shopping, the games, and the gossip in Austen's letters provide readers with a window into the middle class society of her day. She was twenty years old when the letters began, and she continued to write them for twenty-one years until her death.

The different kinds of humor in the correspondence provide some insight into the author's state of mind as she wrote. The early letters contain an abundance of high-spirited self-mockery. In one, she thanks her sister for praising her last letter, humorously protesting that "I write only for fame and without any view of pecuniary emolument."[4] In another, she jokes about the wisdom of a decision not to accompany her brother to London for lack of a place to stay: "if the Pearsons were not at home, I should inevitably fall a Sacrifice to the art of some fat Woman who would make me drunk with Small Beer."[5]

When Austen writes from Bath, either as a visitor or as a resident, her humor has a hard edge, reflecting her discomfort in the monied society of that town. She speaks of meeting a Dr. Hall there "in such very deep mourning that either his mother, his wife, or himself must be dead."[6] As Austen becomes progressively less happy with life in Bath, her good-humored self-mockery gives way to mockery of others. Of an evening when she did not enjoy the company, she observes drily, "Mrs. Badcock & two young Women were of the same party, except when Mrs. Badcock thought herself obliged to leave them to run round the room after her drunken Husband. His avoidance, & her pursuit, with the probable intoxication of both, was an amusing scene."[7]

During her years in Southampton, Austen's humor fluctuates with her spirits. Sometimes she is happy and flip, sometimes cruel. An impersonal mockery often enters her letters: "What is become of all the Shyness in the World? Moral as well as Natural Diseases disappear in the progress of time, & new ones take their place. Shyness & the Sweating Sickness have given way to Confidence & Paralytic Complaints."[8] After 1809, when Austen is once again in Hampshire, her growing self-confidence and success are evidenced in more lighthearted wit. "I must leave off being young," she writes jokingly to Cassandra after attending a social event.[9] Reflecting her contentment, Austen's letters during her last years again exude the happy promise of her youth.

In the end, Austen's letters disappoint readers not because there is too much dry humor in them, but because there is not enough humor of any kind. For every joke or witty turn of phrase, there are ten references to clothing. The author, who rarely mentioned attire in her novels, seems fixated upon it in her letters. Bonnets, gloves, dresses, and cloaks constantly intrude into the lines of Austen's correspondence. These references may simply indicate that fashion, rather than literature or politics, was that about which Cassandra most enjoyed hearing. More likely, however, the repeated mention of clothing indicates how little money the Austen family had to spend on such luxuries and how keenly the author felt this lack. Their not being fashionably dressed only advertised the Austen sisters' modest circumstances to the world. If Austen had had enough money to fill her closets with dresses and bonnets, she probably would not have filled her letters with them.

Not surprisingly, the author's most literary letters are those written after her move to Chawton when she was a published author. Delighting in the praise and the attention her work was receiving, she becomes expansive. She discusses details surrounding the publication of her books with Cassandra and gives advice on literary technique to a niece and nephew who, in emulation of her, are trying their hands at fiction. On separate occasions during these years, she refers to *Sense and Sensibility* and *Pride and Prejudice* as her children. The metaphor suggests that her successful writing career gave Austen a satisfaction equal to that gained by her heroines in their successful marriages.

If one were to single out the ten most important Austen letters, few, if any, would be those written to Cassandra. What Austen writes to her nieces and nephew while she is living at Chawton is what readers and critics have come to value most. She is more open with these intelligent young people than she is with her sister. To them she is less a family member than a literary personage for whom they have considerable respect. They ask her for both literary and personal advice, and she answers them with charm and candor.

In 1814, Austen's niece Fanny wrote to ask whether she should marry a certain suitor. Her aunt responded with two cautious and thoughtful letters that sound very much like her fiction. First she remarks that "Anything is to be preferred or endured rather than marrying without Affection."[10] Two weeks later, she reiterates, "nothing can be compared to the misery of being bound *without* Love, bound to one & preferring another. *That* is a punishment which you do *not* deserve."[11] Two years later, Fanny was still seeking her aunt's advice on matters of the heart. At that time, Austen spoke both hard truths and optimistic encouragement: "Single Women have a dreadful propensity for being poor—which is one very strong argument in favor of Matrimony, but I need not dwell on such arguments with *you*, pretty Dear, you do not want inclination. Well, I shall say, as I have often said before, the right Man will come at last."[12]

Besides advice on how to act, Austen offered literary criticism to her niece Anna and her nephew James Edward, both of whom were beginning to write fiction. She encouraged James Edward by treating him as a colleague and by expressing playful envy of his style:

Uncle Henry writes very superior sermons. You & I must try to get hold of one or two, & put them in our Novels; it would be a fine help to a volume, & we could make our heroine read it aloud of a Sunday Evening.... By the bye, my dear Edward, I am quite concerned for the loss your mother mentions in her Letter; two Chapters & a half to be missing is monstrous! It is well that I have not been at Steventon lately, & therefore cannot be suspected of purloining them; two strong twigs & a half towards a Nest of my own, would have been something.[13]

To her niece, she gave minute criticism and generous praise, indicating her own taste for verisimilitude and precision. Responding to Anna's tendency to move her characters around, Austen suggests, "you had better not leave England. Let the Portmans go to Ireland, but as you know nothing of the Manners there, you had better not go with them. You will be in danger of giving false representations."[14]

An 1815 letter to the Prince Regent's Chaplain, James Stanier Clarke, is one of the few surviving documents written by the author to someone not in the family. Affording the reader a rare glimpse of Austen as she addresses an outsider, it is a marvel of politeness and subtle mockery. In its richness of subtext, it is reminiscent of several letters that appear in the author's fiction. Austen accepts Clarke's praise of her novels which she says she is "too vain" to believe have been "praised beyond their merits," and then politely rejects his suggestion that she write a novel with a clergyman as the principal character. Candidly citing her inability to reproduce men's conversation on such subjects as science and philosophy, Austen nevertheless allows that she "might be equal to" the comic part. As she continues, her sincerity attenuates into a self-confident mockery of herself as a woman and, by implication, of Clarke as a vain man:

A classical education, or at any rate a very extensive acquaintance with English literature, ancient and modern, appears to me quite indispensable for the person who would do any justice to your clergyman; and I think I may boast myself to be, with all possible vanity, the most unlearned and uninformed female who ever dared to be an authoress.[15]

She did not believe this last part; she wrote it only to deflate the self-important chaplain who had suggested that she write a book celebrating someone like himself.

After reading Austen's letters to Clarke and to her nieces and nephew, one understands what her correspondence might have become. In the last years of her life, the author and the family member were beginning to merge into one person. If Austen had lived another twenty years and continued to write, a very different corpus of letters would almost inevitably have emerged. Her early death deprived the literary world both of more wise, witty novels and of dozens of commensurately interesting letters.

Afterword:
The Austen Phenomenon

New trends in literary criticism have fixed Austen more firmly than ever in the pantheon of great writers. Her novels lend themselves as readily to the feminist criticism of Sandra Gilbert and Susan Gubar's *The Madwoman in the Attic*[1] as to James Boyd White's deconstruction of legal and literary texts, *When Words Lose Their Meaning*.[2] Instead of uncovering Austen's shortcomings, new ways of looking at literature seem to illuminate her depth. Reevaluations of the traditional literary canon that are now in progress pose little threat to the Austen oeuvre.

Happily, Austen's work seems to generate high quality literary criticism. Nothing said about her is ridiculous; it is as if her own good sense and irony have kept her critics' minds sharp and reasonable. However, what is written about Austen's novels, like the plots she creates, is disturbing in its very coherence. The works are cogently circumscribed, but the total felicity of the solutions remains slightly disturbing and unconvincing. In the world of Austen's fiction, what one grasps is always intelligible but never complete, and so it is with criticism about her work. As a result, the reader returns with fascination and anticipation to yet another perusal of the novels.

Austen's presence in the contemporary imagination has gone far beyond the scholarly. References to her works now appear in newspaper articles about successful women[3] and on oddball lists such as Noël Coward's assessment of what constitutes style—"A candy-striped Jeep; Jane Austen; Cassius Clay; the *Times* before it changed."[4] Austen is dramatized on television, mentioned in cookbooks, pictured on T-shirts. These seemingly trivial manifestations indicate how deeply Austen's writings have become rooted into the vocabulary and the culture of the English-speaking world. Her influence lies on the surface and in the depths—deceptively accessible and dizzyingly profound.

Notes

Chapter 1   Family and Fiction I: Austen's Life

1. R. W. Chapman, ed., *Jane Austen: Selected Letters 1796–1817* (New York: Oxford University Press, 1985) no. 140 (20 February 1817).
2. James Edward Austen-Leigh, *Memoir of Jane Austen,* reprint of 1871 edition, ed. R. W. Chapman (Oxford: Clarendon Press, 1963), 1.
3. Ibid., 1–2.
4. Chapman, *Selected Letters,* [no number] (July 1817).
5. Joan Rees, *Jane Austen: Woman and Writer* (New York: St. Martin's Press, 1976), 45–46.
6. Quoted in Park Honan, *Jane Austen: Her Life* (New York: St. Martin's Press, 1987), 103.
7. Chapman, *Selected Letters,* no. 11 (17 November 1798).
8. Ibid., no. 70 (25 April 1811).
9. Honan, *Jane Austen: Her Life,* 289.
10. Ibid., 287.
11. Ibid., 123.
12. R. W. Chapman, ed., *Jane Austen's Letters to Her Sister Cassandra and Others,* second edition (London: Oxford University Press, 1933) no. 21 (11 June 1799).
13. Chapman, *Selected Letters,* no. 76 (29 January 1813).
14. Ibid., no. 76 (29 January 1813).
15. Honan, *Jane Austen: Her Life,* 325.
16. Chapman, *Selected Letters,* no. 141 (13 March 1817).
17. R. W. Chapman, ed., *The Works of Jane Austen,* vol. 5, (London: Oxford University Press, 1933), 13.
18. Honan, *Jane Austen: Her Life,* 328–29.
19. Chapman, *The Works of Jane Austen,* vol. 6, 431.
20. Ibid., 433.
21. Sir Walter Scott, "Emma," *Quarterly Review,* 14 (1815): 188–201.
22. Austen-Leigh, *Memoir,* reprint, 132.

Chapter 2   Technique and Theme in Austen's Novels

1. R. W. Chapman, ed., *Selected Letters 1796–1817*, no. 100 (9 September 1814).
2. Ibid., no. 134 (16 December 1816).
3. Scott, *Quarterly Review*, 14 (1815): 188–201.
4. Dr. Anya Taylor, professor of English, John Jay College, New York City, at the Manhattan College Dante Seminar, November 19, 1987.

Chapter 5   *Pride and Prejudice:* The Need for Society

1. R. W. Chapman, ed., *Selected Letters 1796–1817*, no.77 (4 February 1813).

Chapter 9   *Lady Susan, The Watsons,* and *Sanditon:* Framing Austen's World

1. James Edward Austen-Leigh, *Memoir of Jane Austen*, reprint, 364.

Chapter 10   Family and Fiction II: Juvenilia and Letters

1. James Edward Austen-Leigh, *Memoir of Jane Austen*, reprint, 59–60.
2. William and Richard Arthur Austen-Leigh, *Jane Austen: Her Life and Letters: A Family Record* (New York: Dutton, 1913), 82.
3. Ibid., 83.
4. R. W. Chapman, *Jane Austen: Selected Letters 1796–1817*, no. 2 (14 January 1796).
5. Ibid., no. 7 (18 September 1796).
6. Ibid., no. 19 (17 May 1799).
7. Ibid., no. 36 (12 May 1801).
8. Ibid., no. 49 (8 February 1807).
9. Ibid., no. 91 (6 November 1813).
10. Ibid., no. 103 (18 November 1814).
11. Ibid., no. 106 (30 November 1814).
12. Ibid., no. 141 (13 March 1817).
13. Ibid., no. 134 (16 December 1816).
14. Ibid., no. 98 (10 August 1814).
15. Ibid., no. 120 (11 December 1815).

Afterword

1. Sandra Gilbert and Susan Gubar, *The Madwoman in the Attic* (New Haven: Yale University Press, 1979), 107–83.
2. James Boyd White, *When Words Lose Their Meaning: Constitutions and Reconstitutions of Language, Character, and Community* (Chicago: University of Chicago Press, 1984), 163–91.
3. Karen Heller, "You Can Have It All." *Daily News* 27 December 1988, 24.
4. Robert F. Kiernan, *Noel Coward* (New York: Ungar, 1986), 159.

Selected Bibliography

Primary Sources and Biographies

Austen-Leigh, James Edward. *Memoir of Jane Austen,* reprint of 1871 edition. Ed. R. W. Chapman. Oxford: Clarendon Press, 1963.

Chapman, R. W., ed. *The Works of Jane Austen.* 6 vols. London: Oxford University Press, 1925–54.

———, ed. *Jane Austen: Selected Letters 1796–1817.* New York: Oxford University Press, 1985.

Halperin, John. *Life of Jane Austen.* Baltimore: Johns Hopkins University Press, 1984.

Honan, Park. *Jane Austen: Her Life.* New York: St. Martin's Press, 1987.

Rees, Joan. *Jane Austen: Woman and Writer.* New York: St. Martin's Press, 1976.

Critical Works about Jane Austen

Brown, Julia P. *Jane Austen's Novels.* Cambridge: Harvard University Press, 1979.

Butler, Marilyn. *Jane Austen and the War of Ideas.* Oxford: Clarendon Press, 1975.

Chapman, R. W. *Jane Austen: Facts and Problems.* Oxford: Clarendon Press, 1948.

Duckworth, Alistair. *The Improvement of the Estate.* Baltimore: Johns Hopkins University Press, 1971.

Gilbert, Sandra and Susan Gubar. "Inside the House of Fiction: Jane Austen's Tenants of Possibility." In *The Madwoman in the Attic.* New Haven: Yale University Press, 1979, 107–83.

Hardy, Barbara. *A Reading of Jane Austen.* New York: New York University Press, 1976.

Kirkham, Margaret. *Jane Austen, Feminism, and Fiction.* Totowa, New Jersey: Barnes and Noble, 1983.

Lascelles, Mary. *Jane Austen and Her Art*. New York: Oxford University Press, 1939.

Litz, A. Walton. *Jane Austen: A Study of Her Artistic Development*. London: Chatto & Windus, 1965.

McMaster, Juliet, ed. *Jane Austen's Achievement*. New York: Barnes and Noble, 1976.

Monaghan, David, ed. *Jane Austen in a Social Context*. Totowa, New Jersey, 1981.

Mooneyham, Laura. *Romance, Language, and Education in Jane Austen's Novels*. New York: St. Martin's, 1988.

Morris, Ivor. *Mr. Collins Considered*. New York: Routledge, Kegan, & Paul, 1987.

Mudrick, Marvin. *Jane Austen: Irony As Defense and Discovery*. Berkeley, California: University of California Press, 1952.

Poovey, Mary. *The Proper Lady and the Woman Writer*. Chicago: University of Chicago Press, 1984.

Smith, L. P. *Jane Austen and the Drama of Woman*. New York; St. Martin's Press, 1983.

Southam, B. C. *Jane Austen's Literary Manuscripts: A Study of the Novelist's Development through the Surviving Papers*. London: Oxford University Press, 1964.

———. *Jane Austen: The Critical Heritage*. New York: Barnes and Noble, 1968.

Tanner, Tony. *Jane Austen*. Cambridge: Harvard University Press, 1986.

Todd, Janet, ed. *Jane Austen: New Perspectives*. New York: Holmes and Meier, 1983.

Woolf, Virginia. "Jane Austen." In *The Common Reader*. London: 1925.

Index